KONSEP BOOKS
KONSEP LAGENDA SDN BHD
Kuala Lumpur 59100
MALAYSIA
FAX: 282 1348

Konsep Lagenda Sdn Bhd

ISBN 983 9778 04 8

First published November 1996
Second printing March 1997
Third printing September 1997

Cover Design: L. Too
Type set by Konsep Lagenda Sdn Bhd

Printed by
Ritz Print Sdn Bhd

DRAGON MAGIC

My feng shui stories

Prosperity secrets of the living earth
Feng shui stories of the Forbidden City
Stories of modern feng shui

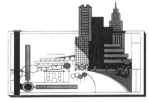

LILLIAN TOO

FULLY ILLUSTRATED
With 16 pages of color photographs

Other books by the author
PUBLISHED BY KONSEP LAGENDA SDN BHD
Feng Shui
Applied Pa Kua Lo Shu Feng Shui
Practical Applications of Feng Shui
Chinese Numerology in Feng Shui
Water Feng Shui for Wealth
Chinese Astrology for Romance and Relationships
The Chinese Dragon
Strategies for Career Success
Creative Visualization
Tap the Power Inside You
Explore the Frontiers of your Mind

Audio Cassettes by the author:
Creative Visualization
Developing Success habits
Positive Affirmations
Making your First Million

PUBLISHED BY ELEMENT BOOKS U.K
The Complete Illustrated Guide to Feng Shui.

PUBLISHED BY BERITA PUBLISHERS
Making your First Million

DRAGON MAGIC
My feng shui stories

Opening Notes

CLOSING NOTES

CONTENTS
Opening notes

THE FENG SHUI MASTER & HIS STORIES

MY PERSONAL FENG SHUI STORIES

CONTENTS

CONTENTS

OPENING NOTES

How did the UK Cosmopolitan magazine put it?
They said it was "*massive in the States, huge Down Under and as common as chopsticks in Hong Kong*" What were they talking about? Feng Shui of course! In a big story devoted to the rise and rise of feng shui, the magazine reported that many celebrities have jumped onto the feng shui bandwagon ... people like Richard Branson, the flamboyant founder of Virgin Records and Virgin Airlines; Boy George the pop singer whose love life was disastrous until he got the feng shui man in, the all time star and writer Shirley Maclaine who had to bring in the feng shui man to re arrange her furniture as her life was getting too cluttered!

Here in Malaysia and Singapore, people *know* about feng shui. Business tycoons use it; as do managers and executives, singers and housewives ... ambitious career types, love starved singles and down to earth grandmothers! Except for a long time, the practice of feng shui festered as a dark secret in the closet ‑ outwardly dismissed as superstition, yet discreetly used. Widely practiced but not openly acknowledged ... until recent years!

Today, the science of feng shui has become respectable, even trendy, due to a global resurgence of interest in things metaphysical. Subjects that are collectively termed *New Age*. In the midst of this explosion of interest in feng shui, it is easy to get carried away by the rhetoric, and lose sight of feng shui's fundamentals and philosophy. The Feng Shui counselor has become much sought after, and there are now many *feng shui masters* offering advisory services. Good feng shui masters are worth their weight in gold, and there are those I revere and respect greatly, because they are well schooled in the fundamentals and also because they are so experienced. And so genuine and humble ... but not all are like that, so if you have only recently discovered feng shui, do be discerning ....

The stories that follow tell of people whose lives, like mine, have been enhanced, or made easier with feng shui inputs. They are *not* part of my dossier of feng shui clients, because I am *not* a feng shui consultant. These are stories from the past and the present. They are contemporary and old, modern and ancient and they each offer valuable insights into the way feng shui works.

Woven into the stories of this book are narratives of my personal study of feng shui, and looking back, it seems like an Odyssey, an intimate experience of discovery into the prosperity secrets of the living earth.

It has been an indulgence in nostalgia writing this book, sharing my experiences and my pictures .... I hope you enjoy my stories, and come away with a greater appreciation of feng shui. ....

Lillian Too.
October 1996

For Jennifer

THE SCIENCE OF FENG SHUI
with **LILLIAN TOO** on Internet
http://www.asiaconnect.com.my/lillian-too

THE GEOMANCER on Internet
http://www.wwwmktg.com/client/feng-shui/

THE FENG SHUI MASTER & HIS STORIES

CHAPTER 1
SO MANY SUCCESS STORIES ...

If I related every case history and described every instance of feng shui's *dragon magic* at work, I could easily fill several volumes. Feng shui operates at so many levels, and in such a variety of distinctive ways for different people, there is little doubt such tales would add layers of new spun perspectives to its practice. It will seem like I was describing something mysterious and magical.

And it would not be *magic* at all.

For feng shui is based on specific guidelines and formulas. Get it right, and you will have tapped into the earth's beneficial energies. Get it wrong, and the energies that surround your space will have become injurious. The key is to diagnose feng shui problems correctly, and having done that to institute correct counter measures. This takes care that *bad vibes* get dissolved, deflected and defeated.

To create good feng shui, it is a simple enough matter to use formulas and methods that operate according to the laws of *yin yang* equilibrium, and *five element* balance, in the process making use of symbolic representations contained in the Pa Kua's eight sides and the Lo Shu's nine squares.

All of this makes up the technology of feng shui. It is a complex discipline and its reach and depth require serious study. But it works, and it is potent. It is something worth learning.

Consider a few lucid examples ...
Let me start by telling you how I set about making my old home come alive once again with potent *sheng chi* after returning to Kuala Lumpur. This time it was no longer success or prosperity that concerned me as much as activating our *descendant's luck.* I was looking to enhance my family's togetherness, and the focus was now on my daughter.

I wanted her to enjoy great good fortune, to have wonderful opportunities open up for her. I wanted her to attain heights of achievement in her studies, and I wanted her to grow up balanced and secure. So feng shui changes were made accordingly, and extensions made to the house were carefully calculated to ensure no missing corners got created, especially corners that affected her well being.

In feng shui, every corner of the house symbolizes some aspect of good fortune and it is important that as extensions are added, any shift in the compass direction sectors are taken account of. This helps to make sure missing sectors do not inadvertently get created, or if they are, to deal with them according to feng shui precepts.

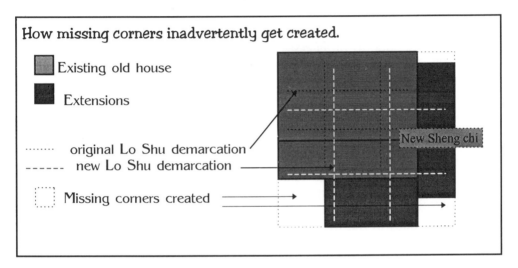

How missing corners inadvertently get created.

Existing old house

Extensions

········ original Lo Shu demarcation

------ new Lo Shu demarcation

Missing corners created

New Sheng chi

Thus we put in additional living areas, as well as a huge new garage, which in effect, caused Jennifer's room to become located in her best *sheng chi* location. This would ensure that she benefits from having her bedroom in her best location.

Then, because the West sector of the house represents the family's *descendants luck*, I chopped down trees that had been planted there when we first moved in. Over the years these trees had grown tall and thick with foliage, so that the sun was completely blocked off. These trees had not been trimmed in all the years I had been away, and I could see that in blocking off the sun, the West sector of my home had become extremely *yin*, and badly needed *yang* energy.

main house

trees on West side gets chopped

If trees are allowed to overgrow and thus overwhelm the house, the sector affected will create misfortune in the area of life which that sector represents. In our case since it was the west, the luck affected would be children's luck. I thus definitely have to keep those trees under control.

In my daughter's bedroom, I activated the *Northeast* sector with a tiny crystal and arranged her sleeping and sitting directions to also tap her best ie her *sheng chi* direction. The crystal would activate her knowledge corner thereby creating auspicious luck in her studies. Tapping her directions would ensure she would be surrounded by good fortune *chi* each time she slept and everytime she sat down to do her work.

As an interesting aside for parents who wonder whether children's good feng shui continue to be effective when they are away at school or University, the answer is <u>yes.</u> For as long as the family home has a room designated for the child, the feng shui continues to be important. Thus any bad feng shui of the child's bedroom at home will similarly continue to send out bad vibes even when the room is not physically occupied.

Did Jennifer benefit from her good feng shui ? I like to think so. She has had a distinguished school career and has been a model student and daughter. She has grown into a lovely young lady. Some friends of hers who have picked up tips and have applied feng shui to their living spaces, have also benefited; and I have included some of these as personal stories in the third section of this book ...

Stories from Yap Cheng Hai ...
But my family feng shui tales pale into insignificance next to Yap Cheng Hai's more spectacular stories. He has been putting the feng shui right for hundreds of business colleagues and friends for well over a quarter of a century, and is deservedly regarded as a feng shui heavyweight. He surely is a most outstanding feng shui Master.

His clients come from all walks of life. They range from University professors who miss out on promotions year after year and who get elevated after their feng shui gets improved; to cash strapped corporations who enjoy windfall injections of cash after their door orientations get altered; to politicians who experience spectacular revivals of fortune after Yap has been to their homes, as well as all manner of businessmen, from a broad cross section of industries, and size. !

Yap Cheng Hai has had countless outstanding successes. It is impossible to single out the ones that are the most spectacular. But perhaps it can be mentioned that in Malaysia where the Chinese comprise only a third of the whole population, it says much for his credibility and reputation that Yap has also been frequently consulted by business leaders of all races.

His clients know that irrespective of their personal religious beliefs, applying feng shui principles to their homes and offices, does not involve a compromise of either their moral or religious beliefs. This is because he approaches feng shui as a science, rather than as a metaphysical practice. There is no praying involved. Nor is it even necessary for the those who benefit from feng shui to believe in it's efficacy. Feng shui is about arranging the living space and the immediate environment in a way that allows the human *chi* to be in harmony with the environmental *chi.* It is not about anything religious.

Take the case of the Minister

of one of Malaysia's richest States. Six years ago, this gentleman was locked in a political battle with his uncle, who had once been his powerful mentor and who was also the political patriarch of the state. Yap Cheng Hai was invited to take a look at his new house. The consultation was arranged by a close supporter of the Minister who was Yap's close friend.

Yap noted that the Minister's new house had two doors, one faced the river that flowed by the house, and another faced the road. In front of the door that faced the road a fountain had been built. In classical feng shui fashion, Yap strongly advised that the door which faced the river should be used as the main door.

This would tap the river and create auspicious feng shui for the house. Yap had determined that the river was flowing away from the house in the best, most auspicious exit direction, a rare phenomenon indeed.

Using the other door would have ruined the Minister's feng shui, and installing the fountain was without feng shui merit. So they covered the fountain, turning it into a flower bed and used the main door that faced the river. Yap further designed the layout of the minister's house, including recommendations on color schemes and furniture arrangements.

When he went to the minister's office, Yap further discovered that the minister was sitting facing his *six killings* direction. He strongly advised the desk be re oriented.

The minister did not immediately accept the advice, Instead he called for a chair to be placed facing the direction Yap had recommended, and sat there without saying a word.

After what seemed like a very long time but in fact was only about fifteen minutes, the minister got up, smiled broadly and ordered the desk to be repositioned. He said he did feel better sitting that way.

Telephone and computer wires had to be pulled out and reinstalled. Carpets had to be moved, but the minister, having decided to go with the feng shui advice, in effect went all the way !

Needless to say, he successfully resolved his political problems with his uncle, and remains as successful a politician today as he ever was then, in fact, more popular than ever. And he has also brought great benefits to his state, for of course that is also the way feng shui works. When a leader's feng shui is good, those he leads also benefits from his good feng shui.

Two hotshot stockbrokers who made it BIG ...
Next, take the case of two clever professionals who turned entrepreneurs. Malaysia's largest and probably most successful home grown stock broking firm was started by two partners, one an American trained fund manager who was Malay, the other a Chinese, an ambitious young remisier, who rose from the ranks of the trading floor. When they formed the partnership in the early Eighties, they were occupying the tenth floor of the Pernas Building.

Yap Cheng Hai was known to the Chinese partner, and was brought in to advise on the arrangement of furniture in the offices of the two partners, as well as the desk positions of the dealers in the trading room. Yap Cheng Hai went to a great deal of trouble to ensure that their overall office feng shui was correct. The partnership took off from day one, and it would be true to say that these two gentlemen never looked back.

Several years later when they came upon the opportunity to buy their own building, they invited Yap Cheng Hai to check out the feng shui of the building. It was during the recession years and the building was going cheap. Yap did not like the building. He strongly advised against the purchase.

But they insisted, reluctant to let the opportunity go; so Yap made five trips in all ... to see what could be done to correct the feng shui of the building. Finally he told the partners, *Buy it by all means but you have to spend several million dollars to make important changes.* Systematically he listed the changes that needed to be made.

The original main entrance was too narrow, he told them, *and too low.*

The *chi* could not breath. So the main door would have to be extended ten, maybe fifteen feet. The door also had to be raised, made taller. And its direction had to be changed, but ever so slightly, that it is hardly noticeable.

And then in front of the door to balance the busy flow of traffic on the main road which the building faced, Yap told them to *build an artificial fountain, not the cascading type but the one with the water flowing inwards towards the building.*

The signboard which had been placed below the door level was also demolished, and in its place, a new signboard was erected at the top of the building. Having the signboard below the entrance level was bad feng shui. Placing it proudly at the top of the building was good feng shui.

Inside the building, the desk orientations of both partners, as well as the dealers in the dealing room were worked out. He took special care that the desks of both partners was properly aligned according to their individual birth dates. The Malay partner was quite happy to go with Yap's advice. Not knowing anything about feng shui he was quite happy as long as the arrangement made good aesthetic sense. The Chinese partner however kept changing his sitting direction. This not only caused imbalance in his office but it was to cause a fallout between the two partners.

Today RHB is Malaysia's largest stock broking company. It is also the most profitable. The Malay partner, Tan Sri Rashid Hussein continues to be one of Malaysia's most highly respected stockbroker, and indeed, he is more than just a stockbroker, being now the controlling force behind a financial conglomerate which comprise institutions engaged in a broad spectrum of commercial and investment banking activities. The Chinese partner, Chua Ma Yu has sold out his share and gone on to other business ventures.

But both have benefited from Yap Cheng Hai's feng shui expertise.

Chua's Waterfront project in the Philippines
has also been arranged according to feng shui advice by Yap Cheng Hai. His casino hotel project in Cebu in the Philippines which has been listed on the Manila stock exchange, for example was built according to feng shui guidelines.

7

The hotel has been a success from the start, and when the company went public, its shares soared to levels which have seen Chua more than triple the value of his investment.

Closer home, Yap continues to be tycoon Chua's feng shui mentor. In the early days when Chua built his residence in the elite Bangsar/Pantai hill suburb of Kuala Lumpur, the slope and shape of the land had presented a challenge.

The main door had to be tilted to ensure that the higher ground was on the left, *thereby making it symbolize the dragon*, and not the tiger. Since those days, Chua's bank account has soared, and he is today one of Malaysia's many multi millionaire tycoons. Needless to say Yap continues to design the feng shui of his other property development projects scattered around Kuala Lumpur and in Labuan where Chua also has investments.

Advising Top Bankers ...

Yap Cheng Hai is particularly respected by many of Malaysia's top bankers. He has advised countless bank managers and general managers, and perhaps two of his most highly respected friends who have benefited from his feng shui advice are Chairman of Public Bank, Tan Sri Thong Yaw Hong, and Chairman of Pacific Bank Tan Sri Dr. Lin See Yan.

Both men have had highly distinguished careers with the Government, Tan Sri Thong was for many years the head of the Government's Economic Planning Unit and Director General of the Finance Ministry while Tan Sri Dr. Lin was also for many years the Deputy Governor of Malaysia's Central Bank.

That they believe in feng shui says much for their broadminded attitudes towards an ancient practice, that is also a part of their Chinese cultural heritage. It would be foolish to declare that their distinguished careers were due entirely to feng shui luck, for they are brilliant men in their own right. But every career has its ups and downs, and it would not be untrue to say that during their periods of *low heaven luck*, feng shui would have helped them overcome difficult times. Indeed, when a new governor took over at the Central Bank a couple of years ago, and the Central Bank itself was going through a period of bad press caused by large foreign exchange losses, Yap was brought in to arrange the desk orientation of the new Governor. This was to ensure that the incoming Governor would have a smoother reign than his predecessor.

Yap Cheng Hai has also told me that once he was invited to Hong Kong by someone very senior in the Ka Wah Bank there many years ago. At that time Ka Wah Bank was still afloat, but when he checked out the feng shui of the offices of the Bank's Managing Director and other Directors, he had discovered so many things wrong that he had strenuously warned them.

Unfortunately, the luckless Lau brothers had ignored his advice and dismissed the suggested changes as *too much trouble*. Not soon after, Ka Wah Bank collapsed, and the brothers themselves fled to Taiwan.

In this case, Yap is convinced their *Heaven luck* was so bad it was beyond help, and their intentions had not been honorable, and so they were meant for an ignominious fall.

Property Developers get feng shui advice ..

In Malaysia, feng shui is now so widely respected that few property developers will launch any project without the feng shui master's inputs. Yap Cheng Hai is regularly consulted by many of the country's more prominent property tycoons ... people like Tan Sri Wan Azmi of Land and General whose old office in Kampung Bahru and whose new mansion in Ampang benefited from Yap's feng shui inputs. Land and General is presently successfully building an impressive new township on the outskirts of Kuala Lumpur.

Yap's inputs are usually brought in during the design stages of any project, and he is fond of pointing out successful shopping malls, housing estates and factories whose feng shui has been improved by him. I suspect he gets much satisfaction, and takes great pride in his expertise, each time he observes his efforts succeed

A recent development he consulted for is the hugely successful new township of Bandar Utama, yet another new suburb of Kuala Lumpur. Built by veteran developers Paramount Group, and owned by the Teo family, the showcase of this development is a huge shopping mall, One Utama, which was an instant success when it opened a few months previously. Yap tilted the entrance several degrees to the right to capture the Teo patriarch's best direction. Buildings next to the mall, also owned by the same family, and which houses the country's TV3 television company, had their corners cut off as one of these edges had been directly pointed at the company's marketing and sales office.

See sketch below.

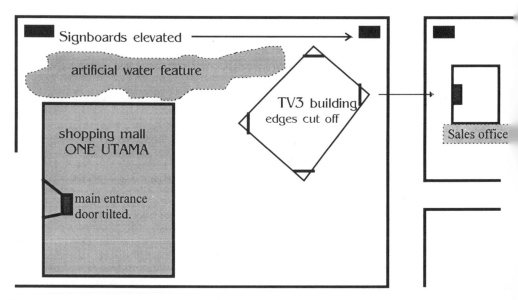

There is presently a building boom around the country, and corporations engaged in property development increasingly use good feng shui as much as a competitive tool, as to ensure smooth business.

The number of feng shui masters has mushroomed accordingly, and to my surprise, I discover this is not only in Malaysia and Singapore, but also in the Western countries as well.

Interest in feng shui is on the rise, as more of the world's thinking peoples realize that from the Middle Kingdom that is ancient China, has come a revival of a very old practice that is surprisingly very relevant to the modern world's concerns with the environment.

That feng shui's invisible dragon's breath relates so closely to the scientific harnessing of the earth's now discernible energy lines makes the practice all the more tantalizing and exciting.

I have long maintained that knowledge of feng shui is a valuable additional tool for life and living, if nothing else to ensure that all new man made structures built by the world's Governments and corporations are done so with an eye to living in harmony with the environment. The extent of feng shui's growing influence is thus very welcome indeed.

Feng Shui and the environment

Much of feng shui's guidelines overlap the concerns of environmentalists. Like them, feng shui strongly advise against *injuring the dragon* when clearing land for development.

Exposed soil suggest a wounded dragon; Haphazard structures cause imbalance and send out *killing breath* in all directions. Buildings that are not properly landscaped similarly cause disparity of the elements. There could be an excess of *yin or yang* energies created. Or the five elements are combined in a destructive fashion that attracts bad luck.

Feng shui speaks of polluted rivers and drains with trepidation. Stagnant waters are said to cause *bad chi,* and fast moving waters made heavy with exposed soil create grave misfortunes. Mankind is warned against living near such places.

Too much heat from the sun causes an excess of yang energy so that global warming caused by cracks in the world's ozone layer could create too much *yang* energy for the earth. Likewise, excess cold and humidity cause there   to be an excess of *yin* energy. Too much of yin or yang cause imbalance which provokes the dragon fury.

Thus do the Chinese explain natural disasters like earthquakes and floods, typhoons and volcanic eruptions as reflecting the intense wrath of the dragon. This creature's displeasure, when brought to a pitch, often cause massive destruction. Nothing hurts like the dragon's passionate fury.

When rivers break their banks, it is the *water dragon* that is angered. When storms bring death and destruction it is the *wind dragon* demonstrating his great displeasure. And when the earth cracks open or mountains spew forth fire and brimstone, it is the *fire dragon* raging at being disturbed.

Live in harmony with the earth's landscapes ...

and feng shui offers the promise of great prosperity and happiness for generations ... it has taken me almost a lifetime to truly understand the dragon symbolism of the ancient texts, and to unlock the superstitious declarations of my ancestors ... Seen in retrospect, my years in Hong Kong, and my subsequent retirement from a colorful corporate career that was peppered with highs and lows seem now to be itself a journey of sorts, one that allows me to systematically unlock the cryptic workings of feng shui and learn the prosperity secrets of the living earth.

When I returned to Malaysia in the early Nineties and looked around for a meaningful occupation to fill the hours of my waking days, events directed me towards a writing career. The notes I had made through the years became valuable research papers, and my great friend and si fu, Yap Cheng Hai became my feng shui mentor, someone I had easy access to when I needed to check on the more complex aspects of feng shui practice.

But Yap Cheng Hai was to play a greater role than merely being a source of reference. He became actively involved in the process of methodically putting together the valuable guidelines of feng shui. Inspired by the thought of collating this valuable body of knowledge into books and make feng shui forever available to everyone, Yap dug out old manuscripts and notebooks that had been given to him years earlier. He found them in forgotten boxes tucked behind cupboards.

Yap's notebooks were already yellow with age, the paper brittle and dry, when he brought them to my home. The tiny handwritten words had to be read with a magnifying glass. The old language couched in arcane metaphors had to be re interpreted and the meanings of the old formulas had to be unlocked. So we worked together, often through the night and into the early hours of the morning.

Each time there was ambiguity or doubt, the solution would present itself only after much discussion and debate, but when this happened the particular rule or guideline became blazingly clear. Those were moments of sheer delight and undiluted pleasure, as we penetrated the veil of the old language and understood the symbolism locked within the ancient words.

Yap took it upon himself to painstakingly explain background stories and legends that gave meaning to the phrases. Many of the seemingly strange and cryptic references to stories of other eras and ages made sense to him because he was so well schooled in the Chinese classics and Chinese mythology. And so he not only translated the literal meanings to me, Yap also gave form and substance to the literal translations.

In the process of enhancing my knowledge of feng shui, I have also become more knowledgeable about China's history, its dynastic chain, and much of the village folklore and superstition that surrounds the rise of the founding emperors of China.

Some of these have been included as part of this collection of stories..

It was my job to simplify all that Yap told me and taught me, and supplemented by my own notes of conversations I had also had with other experts; as well as my own research readings, it was not too difficult a process. Yap Cheng Hai also has six very old *luo pans* and these served like guideposts which pointed to yet further references

As we progressed, the process became easier and easier, so that knowledge poured forth like a deluge, and my pen could barely move fast enough to capture all the wonderful stuff that came forth from those late night sessions. In all we spent two years working this way. Already three stunningly valuable feng shui formulas have seen the light of day through books I published for the SE Asian markets, and now through THE COMPLETE ILLLUSTRATED GUIDE TO FENG SHUI published by Element Books of UK, USA and Australia which had its worldwide release in October of this year ... but there is still so much more of feng shui knowledge I have yet to organize into simplified texts.

It is just a matter of time before they get published. In this era when modern communications technology makes everything so easily available to so many, the secrets of the living earth, once symbolized by the Chinese dragon is no longer obscure, no longer hidden. For feng shui knowledge is not disseminated only through books. There are so many web sites on Internet that deal with and offer feng shui services, I can see that indeed feng shui has already *crossed the great waters to other shores,* as the I Ching predicted to me that it would four years ago when I consulted the Oracle before publishing my first book on the subject !

I personally have two web sites managed by two different companies which beam out my feng shui books and articles to the world via Internet. For the information of those amongst you who regularly surf the Net here are my two web site addresses:

1.   http://www.asiaconnect.com.my/lillian-too

2.   http://www.wwwmktg.com/client/feng-shui/

It is obvious that Feng shui is more than a practice in prosperity. It embodies a whole philosophy, and it uses the promise of material well being to entice us, and then in practicing feng shui, we come to develop a deep respect for the winds and waters of the living earth.

The stories contained in this book are a mixture of old and new ... those selected from my store of personal feng shui experiences offer deeper perspectives to the practice of feng shui while those that come from China, both the China of the old days and China of this century ... embody a titillating mix of folklore and village gossip ... collectively they will enhance the reader's appreciation of the nuances of feng shui practice ....

There are also stories that reflect much of my personal odyssey into the wonderful world of *feng shui* ... from the way it touched my life in the early years, slowly seeping into my consciousness until it became a passion, to the unexpected unraveling of its secret formulas to me, and through me to the world .... The process took many years, much of it coloured by a series of milestone events and developments, some signifying tremendous good fortune, and others manifesting the dangers of intense bad luck.

It will become obvious to the reader as you turn the pages that good and bad luck often comes in many different guises, and it is only later when you look back at events with the benefit of hind sight, that you can begin to detect the patterns that mark turning points ... only then does it become possible to decipher the meaning of things read and knowledge gained.

I was never a conventional student of feng shui; everything I know about the subject has been distilled from years of practicing it under a variety of scenarios and seeing it work for me ... and for others. A great deal of reading, and endless discussions with very knowledgeable people has added sum and substance to these experiences. I was *luckier* than most because as I moved through the different stages of my life, I was to meet just exactly the right people, at the right time, who would either themselves provide the key to unlocking fresh new insights, or they would introduce me to experts who possessed the answers to my questions.

It was during the Hong Kong years that my exposure to feng shui attained stunning heights, although I was not truly aware of it as it happened. Living in this highly superstitious environment where almost everything is explained in terms of feng shui, it is easy to get carried away by the superficialities of the science. Luckily for me I am also an avid reader, and I am not one to accept banal explanations that roll glibly off the tongues of those who would seek to commercialize an ancient science ...
Neither am I the gullible sort.

But I was a keen student, and I was also very good at parlaying my position and my contacts into many valuable trips and meetings that were great *eye openers* for me. Thus, for instance, apart from important business and work, my visits to China also became extremely valuable investigative journeys.

For in China, I had opportunities to meet with and discuss aspects of feng shui theory with a broad cross section of experts that included University professors, museum researchers, architects and scholars.

Some of my most precious insights into the imperial practice of feng shui came from my visits to the Forbidden City in Beijing, where I was privileged to get personally conducted tours. My guides were so knowledgeable and so eager to part with their knowledge that I was to become quite exceedingly inspired to study the history of the Mings and the Chings, the two dynasties that lived and ruled from the City. I was intensely interested in looking for evidence of feng shui inputs that had gone into the architecture of the palaces, mainly because I believed that if the emperors, (who in those days ruled absolutely and who had complete access to all the experts in the land) used feng shui, then definitely feng shui was something very special indeed. I did not have to look very hard.

The whole of the Forbidden City is drenched with symbols and patterns, shapes and decorations, alignments and orientations that demonstrate an almost universal application of feng shui ...

All the symbols of longevity are there. As are massive stone lions which stand guard at every doorway and entrance. Deep in the heart of the Palace Complex the Audience Halls dripped with dragons. This celestial creature symbolizes the power of the emperor, his invincibility, his courage ... his tenacity and his unquestioned authority. The dragon is everywhere, coiled round pillars, carved onto walls, hugging the doors, embracing the ceilings, and most of all gripping the thrones of the emperors ! I was so taken by the dragons that in 1988, in the year of the dragon, and soon after my acquisition of Dragon Seed department store, I wrote a book about the Chinese dragon.

Further inside the heart of the City where the living quarters of the emperors were located, one sees all the objects that symbolize conjugal bliss, longevity and the advent of many descendants ...

If I had to point to a time when my interest in the subject turned genuinely serious, it was probably after my visits to the Forbidden City. For seeing it so spectacularly laid out brought it to life for me. I became quite intoxicated by the colours and the lyrical philosophy of balance and harmony that lay behind the subject.

I discovered Feng Shui to be an extraordinary body of laws and principles whose practice is neither mystical nor mysterious, requiring neither a religious fervor nor an ardent faith. There are no spiritual pre requisites, although those who see only the superficial surface of its practice may be persuaded to think otherwise.

I regard Feng Shui as simply another sort of science that is not based on Western definitions. Instead, Feng shui is grounded on the Chinese view of the Universe which focuses on balance and harmony. Thus *yin* and *yang* cosmic processes and the dynamics of element interactions become important in its practice..

At first however, I was skeptical. My regard for the subject blended curiosity with a certain cynicism. I followed feng shui instructions to change my *sleeping direction* at a time when I was desperate for funds to finance my MBA studies in the United States but only because it cost me nothing to do so. Yet believe it or not, soon after the change, against all odds I actually succeeded in winning a full scholarship to go to the Harvard Business School.

That surprise windfall was followed some years later with (for my husband and I) the almost miraculous arrival of our first and only child. Jennifer came into our lives. We had given up hope of ever having children, and our marriage had gone chronically sour. But after my return from Harvard, we moved house, and amazingly, our relationship experienced the most magical improvement capped the following year with the birth of our child, an event that brought us great joy. That was when I became truly convinced.

In later years I postulated that feng shui practice involved no compromise of any of my values or religious belief. So I continued to consult feng shui experts, and I continued to use its guidelines every time I found myself in need of some additional help or some serious good luck to tide me over some frantic situation, or when I felt impotent with worry.

As the years passed I began to see feng shui in a new light. I started to rationalize myself into treating it as a *science*. I rejected connotations of spirituality in its practice. Instead, I searched for its roots and educated myself on the fundamental concepts on which it based its recommendations and its formulas. And while I did not fully comprehend exactly how feng shui worked, I was prepared to go with the flow ... and to accept that it actually did work. I saw amazing results in the way it helped me cope with difficult times and I saw how it brought me amazing opportunities for personal growth and success during good times.

It was thus that I came to relentlessly pursue all and any knowledge that was related to its many concepts and permutations.
I discovered that the fundamental principle of feng shui is the contention that invisible energy lines swirl about the atmosphere ... The ancient Chinese wise men must somehow have discovered the existence of these invisible energy flows.

Except that they called it the dragon's breathe, *sheng chi* ... or if it was a malignant killing sort of breath they called it *shar chi*. The Chinese have known about the existence of *chi* for thousands of years !

Now of course modern science has also discovered that the atmosphere is indeed crowded with energy lines. There are even instruments to measure these invisible lines, now given scientific names like waves and flows. We have fax machines and mobile phones. televisions and radios.

Radar and satellite stations measure waves in the air. Weather conditions are photographed from high up in the sky, and now we have Internet, the global computer network that links sixty million people or more through satellite transmissions and telephone lines ... these new inventions have suddenly demonstrated the existence of invisible energy forces around us !

I often point out to people that if they take down their TV aerial, in a flash they lose their picture ! Re install the aerial, and tune it right, and the picture comes through bright and clear. Mobile phones let us speak to anyone anywhere in the world. Portable radios bring music to us wherever we are ... how do these sounds and pictures get to us so instantaneously ? How do they reach us ?

Think of feng shui's cosmic *chi*. Is *chi* somehow similar to the invisible transmission waves in the atmosphere ?

Can this intangible *chi* really bring good fortune, and can it really be tapped for protection against bad luck. And can it genuinely bring good luck, thereby affecting the material fortunes of Mankind ?

If the ancient books on feng shui, and what has come down through the generations, are to be believed, the answer to all these questions is a resounding YES !

I believe in feng shui because I have seen it work so many times. All through my career years, feng shui has provided persuasive solutions whenever I took the trouble to arrange my living space according to its precepts. I am not saying it was the be all and end all of my entire career, but when you see how it seemed to always smooth my path for me ... in my work, in my career, in my business and in my family life, you too will begin to share my excitement, and my belief and trust in this knowledge.

Do not be too startled by the uncanny coincidences, *as I was*, when they happened. All my inclinations to correlate cause and effect i.e. feng shui change followed by positive developments that came soon after, had always started out tentative, but later, I really had to conclude that I did enjoy tremendous good fortune and success, and even seemingly divine protection, each time I turned to feng shui for help.

With this narrative therefore, I am inviting you, dear reader, into my humble world, and into my consciousness, where dragons and tigers take on important symbolic meaning.

I am hoping my stories will make the non believer take a second look into this fascinating subject, and to offer those currently investigating it some down to earth insights into its practical aspects.

Feng shui must not be seen as the ultimate remedy for everything that goes wrong. Feng Shui must be placed in its correct perspective. Perhaps I should speak about the trinity of luck. Do remember there are three types of luck, the luck from heaven (*tien chai*); the luck from the earth (*ti chai*) and the luck from mankind himself (*ren chai*).

We cannot control the circumstances under which we are born. Some are born into rich and powerful families, some are born poor. Some people have looks, others have intellect and still others have wealth, to start off with. We have no control over our heaven luck.

But we can, and should control our earth luck and our mankind luck. This is because the luck from the earth comes from feng shui, which comes from living in harmony with the environment. Tap the luck from the earth, and you can balance out all that is lacking in your heaven luck !

In the same way we can also control our mankind luck for this comes from within ourselves. Work hard and persevere, and good earth luck lends us a helping hand. Be careless and lazy, and even the best feng shui will be quite wasted ! Even the most magnificent *sheng chi* will evaporate or stagnate in the midst of negativism and indolence !

So do not expect feng shui to work like magic. Its effect can sometimes seem slow, thereby testing your patience. The speed with which results are seen also depends on many inter related, complex and intangible forces, many of which we still do not yet fully understand.

I believe in feng shui because I am excited by what I believe is *provisional* confirmation of the existence of the *cosmic chi.* I observe the terrific explosion of technological advances currently taking place ... and I am convinced the day will surely come when feng shui's *chi* will be more thoroughly understood by the scientists, and more widely acknowledged by all the communities of the world.

Already, acceptance of feng shui has crossed the great waters, to far away places of the Western world, to Australia and England, to Europe and Canada and the United States. Newspapers and magazines throughout the world increasingly write about the rise and rise of feng shui, and demand for feng shui books continue to grow.

In this Age of Aquarius, knowledge and practice of feng shui seem poised for a very spectacular renaissance indeed.

But first let me take you back to the time when I first met Yap Cheng Hai. Let me introduce you to this feng shui master of our times ...

CHAPTER TWO
MEETING UP WITH YAP CHENG HAI
... a hugely entertaining storyteller of the old school.

Yap Cheng Hai has the most amazing personality. I first met him when I joined his *kung fu* class in the early Seventies. From the start I was mesmerized. I could listen to him the entire night and not be bored. Yap Cheng Hai had an aura of confidence that bordered on arrogance, yet it was a nice kind of arrogance, the type that made you want to learn from him. He was educated in Chinese and could converse easily in seven dialects. Over the years, he had also learnt to speak English, so we had no problems communicating. He told us stories in English but every now and again he would break into Hokkien, his favorite Chinese dialect. Since I spoke Hokkien, I had little difficulty understanding him. In later years when I started collaborating with him on my books, I was to speak Cantonese with him, for by then Cantonese had become my *language of feng shui*, so to speak, having spent so many years discussing the subject with other experts from Hong Kong.

The twice weekly kung fu evenings ...
It was at the kung fu evenings that I first heard about *feng shui*, and over a period of about three years I was to have my eyes opened to the richness and vastness of the Chinese arts and sciences. I was to be persuaded that *feng shui* explained much about mankind's fortunes, and about a family's happiness.

In those days, Yap Cheng Hai seldom got technical with me. That was to come later ... but after our exercise sessions, when all of us adjourned for a late supper of porridge or fried Hokkien noodles in the road side stalls of old town, he would tell us one story after another, about this famous Dato, and that famous tycoon, whose fortunes had soared or waned, according to their good and bad *feng shui*.

Because Yap Cheng Hai is such an eloquent storyteller, I had a hard time taking him seriously. In those days, I was skeptical about anything that bordered on *magic*, or seemed metaphysical.

Besides, because he indulges in so many branches of psychic phenomena and paranormal type activities, I was also wary of him. Yap Cheng Hai was a Buddhist, but he was also a Taoist of the old school.

He was full of stories to tell, and things to show.

He possessed swords and belts and an entire cupboard full of *talismans.* He would claim these had some kind of protective power. Once we were having a light Sunday lunch together and he told me how he had once visited the British Museum in London, and going through the labyrinth of rooms had had a most interesting *conversation* with one of the Mummies there !

Another time, he claimed to have been in the chapel of the Vatican in Rome when he saw St. Peter standing at or near the altar ... I came to the conclusion then that Yap Cheng Hai was definitely a psychic of sorts !

In another era and another society he might well have been a medicine man; or the Chinese equivalent of a *bomoh,* a magician !

I was to find out later, that in harboring those cynical observations about him, I was doing him a great and grave injustice for in the many years I have since known him, Yap Cheng Hai has proven to be the kindest, most generous hearted and honorable of men.

That he had a native curiosity into all things now termed *New Age,* was definite. But there was nothing *mumbo jumbo* or evil about his knowledge, his beliefs or his skills. He was a genuine mystic.

He was also hugely intelligent and forthright. He pursued skills in the Chinese martial arts to an inordinately high degree. Once I saw him defend himself with one finger against a visiting Taiwanese black belt tae-kwon-do expert, making mincemeat out of the poor man, much along the lines of the sort of things you see in Chinese *kung fu* movies of the Bruce Lee or Jackie Chan type !

Except that Yap Cheng Hai did it all with great gusto and a bellyful of laughs. I always told him that he reminded me of the Laughing Buddha, the Maitreya Buddha, especially with his big belly, which he claimed housed his precious *chi,* his internal and intangible strength.

Another time he showed me a penknife that was as sharp as a razor blade and made me cut at his torso. When I refused, he grabbed hold of my hand and sliced it hard against his bared stomach. The knife could not penetrate his skin ! And when I protested that he must have used his special martial arts skill to overcome the blade's effect, in a second he had undid the belt he was wearing around his waist and buckled it round me instead.

And before I knew what was happening, he had grabbed hold of my hand and in a second had sliced several cuts through my arm. Instead of the lines of blood I expected to see, my arm stayed pristine and untouched ! Fabulous stuff !

" *Ha see,*" he laughed triumphantly, " *this belt is from India, very old ... if you wear it, it will protect you forever !* " The belt was however not for sale.

Yap Cheng Hai was always given to the most extravagant of statements. But we were fascinated by every new thing he told us. I, especially loved it all. He was opening a whole new world to me about the beliefs and customs and practices of the East, and I was a very attentive pupil ! But the stories that fascinated me the most were his *feng shui* stories.

Discovering feng shui ...
He told me he had spent some years in Taiwan learning from the most famous feng shui master there, Master <u>Chan Chuan Huay,</u> a man who had created *feng shui* so auspicious for some of the richest men of Taiwan of another era, he had become something of a folk hero.

Master Chan had given him several valuable old books that contained his oldest and most potent formulas ... and two of these have been passed on to me and have now seen the light of day as feng shui books written in the English language !

Master Chan had been the expert on *water feng shui.*
Water flows and their directions, exits and entrances were his great specialty, and Yap Cheng Hai spent the best part of his time in Taiwan apprenticed to Master Chan, learning all about this most valuable branch of feng shui !

But water feng shui was not all that he learnt. His appetite whetted by the valuable formulas given to him, Yap Cheng Hai then proceeded to investigate other schools of feng shui, spending time with the great feng shui masters of Hong Kong and Singapore, some of whom were monks whose knowledge were seldom used commercially, while others made a living out of the science.

In the course of his investigations into feng shui, Yap Cheng Hai visited many grave sites. I thought it absurd to go to such lengths, and told him so, but he was adamant. The most powerful feng shui, he said was the feng shui of ancestral burial grounds.

The Taiwanese practitioners of feng shui, he told me, were especially mindful of the feng shui of their ancestors. The orientation of grave sites, and the quality of their feng shui, they believed, had a direct effect on the fortunes of descendants, especially male descendants. Indeed, in Taiwan, Yap Cheng Hai said, rich families went to great trouble to guard their ancestors graves. And in China, this type of feng shui was used to explain the rise of many of the country's emperors, including the new emperors of this century ... Dr Sun Yat Sen, Mao Tze Tung and Deng Xioa Ping ... stories of their feng shui are part of this collection.

Years later, on one of my visits to China, I had the good fortune to meet with a Master Yang, an old scholar, bent low from permanent injury sustained during the horrendous cultural revolution, who was also deeply knowledgeable about feng shui.

My meeting with him had been arranged by a friend of a friend, and since Master Yang spoke Cantonese, I asked Master Yang about feng shui of grave sites and how important they were to the fortunes of descendants, and he had confirmed what Yap Cheng Hai had told me.

" *But that is the feng shui of yin dwellings ... the houses of the dead ... just as vital, in fact more so is the feng shui of yang dwellings ... the houses of the living* ".

It is for this reason that I have myself focused <u>only</u> on feng shui for *yang* dwellings. Unlike Yap Cheng Hai I have no desire to go trekking over cemeteries and graveyards in search of evidence of the efficacy of *yin* feng shui.

Discovering *chi* ...

Yap Cheng Hai had a martial arts *si fu* or Master called Chee Kim Thong who used to teach *kung fu* to the bodyguards of the Kuomintang generals. Master Chee was an expert in the Shaolin arts, and especially in the *sarm cheen* wu shu type of martial arts. Much of the movements and exercises involved learning how to raise the internal *chi* that lies within the human body.

This was based on the theory that this internal *chi*, or intangible energy was far more effective, far stronger and much more powerful than mere physical strength. In those days, neither Master Chee nor Master Yap could satisfy me with theoretical explanations concerning this *chi*, but later I was to discover that the *chi* of Mankind was based on the concept that the human body was a miniature Universe.

Similar experts in Hong Kong and Taiwan referred to *chi* as the intangible strength that lay within the body, and proper *kung fu* training allows this *chi* to be effectively harnessed by conscientious students who focused their minds when training in the martial arts.

This focused concentration was so potent, it could then teach the body, through a series of exercise movements and meditation, to act and react according to the cosmic law which governs the flow of *chi*.

Tales of the Universal *chi*

Much of my *kung fu* evenings in Yap Cheng Hai's house was spent learning how to capture, and raise this *chi* from within my own body. I discovered that this vital magic breath was impossibly difficult to understand, and even harder to raise ! What I learnt seemed very Taoist, in that the more gentle the movement, the more *chi* it possessed, and thus the more deadly was its potential !

"You see" I remember Yap Cheng Hai telling me, *"the most gentle thing in the world overrides the most hard and the most strong"*, and he would point to examples from nature ... *" consider the effect of water as it flows and wears away at the hard rocks that lie in its path ...."*   Thus did he try to educate me on the flow of *chi* within the human body .... in the process probably also imparting some Tao philosophy.

The human *chi* had to do with the breath, the life force of individuals. In kung fu, the word for breath is *chi*, and probably the best translation of this breath is *vital or intrinsic energy*. When the warrior who is well trained in *kung fu* breathes, he combines spiritual breathing with physical breathing so that the spiritual energy that is centered in the psychic center of the body (referred to as *tan tien*) or subtle *chi* gets activated, giving the warrior tremendous strength and power in his movements. When engaged in combat he will thus be victorious !

The goal of every martial arts student is to perfect the art of raising this vital cosmic *chi* within the body, so I tried to understand its nature as much as I could.

Through our regular exercises I discovered nuances of this *chi*. I found that the more relaxed and natural I was, the more rhythmic and supple my movements became.

And the more graceful my movements became, the more effective and powerful became my strokes,.

So that in exercises where I engaged simulated movements with opponents, I realized that as long as I applied the rhythm of advancing and retreating, of absorbing my opponent's weight and force, the more I seemed to be applying the cosmic principle of *yin and yang* ... thereby creating a balance, a rhythmic dance that allowed me occasionally to actually feel my own *chi* rising, and filling me with the most wondrous kind of vitality !

Each time I tried too hard, the *chi* would get obstructed and literally vanish. I also discovered that sudden and jerky movements quickly dispersed any awareness of the *chi*.

It took me a long time, but slowly I came to realize that as long as my movements were light and graceful, flexible and continuos, relaxed and tranquil, the feeling of energy and vitality would consume me.

It was a beautiful sensation, and it gave me a kind of high I could not at first identify. It was only later that I came to recognize these as moments when *chi* was being created within my body ! I loved the sensation of those moments, and years later, long after I had given up learning *kung fu* I was to remember the intrinsic nature of *chi*.

Manifestations of *chi*, the magic cosmic breath

Central to feng shui is the cosmic breath of the symbolic green dragon, the magic *chi* which exists also in the human body and can be activated through focused meditation and practice; chi exists also in the space and environments around us. Capturing this universal cosmic *chi* is what feng shui is about. Illustrated here are three examples of the manifestation of human *chi*.

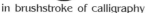

in brushstroke of calligraphy   in the warrior's blow   in meditation

---

Having experienced the human *chi* it was far easier for me to comprehend another more powerful kind of *chi* ... For of course, along the way, Yap Cheng Hai also educated me on this greater and more powerful *chi*, the kind that swirled about our Universe ... he called it *sheng chi*, the Universal breath that brought auspicious good fortune.

The *Chi* of Feng Shui

Effectively and cleverly creating, harnessing and storing this *sheng chi*, he said, was what the ancient science of Feng Shui was all about. " *If your house has plenty of sheng chi,*" he said " *Wah ! ... you will have every kind of happiness ... and you will be so rich ! ".*

But like the breath of kung fu, Yap Cheng Hai told me, there was also another kind of breath, the killing breath or *shar chi.*

Feng Shui strenuously warns against being hit by *shar chi,* for this is the breath that brings misfortunes, loss, even death ! "*Terrible disaster is caused by the pointed breath of shar chi*" Yap Cheng Hai explained. The most common examples of *shar chi* were the pointed, triangular shape of roof lines. Anyone whose main door lies directly facing such a roof line (caused by a neighbor's house for instance) is sure to suffer misfortune of some kind ... it can be an illness, a severe loss of money, a lot of quarrels within the family ... and even death, if the residents of the home are going through a low period.

When Yap Cheng Hai first introduced me to the dangers of being hit by *shar chi,* he would point out these roof lines to me and whenever we came across a house whose door appeared to be hit by just such a roof line, he would excitedly ask me to notice how, even the grass could not grow ... and it was indeed so ...these houses invariably looked run down and very sad indeed !

Then he told me about the classical taboo of the T junction. " *You must never have your house, and especially the main front door directly facing an oncoming road,* " he told us solemnly one night, vigorously shaking his head for emphasis, " *the lights from oncoming cars are like tigers rushing in to kill you !* "

And as with the case of the roof lines, he pointed out all sorts of examples to me, and once again those houses placed dramatically in the path of the malignant tigers looked faded and very down and out.

Until one day we saw a house in Klang which belonged to a friend of his, a woman who ran a successful restaurant and to all intents and purposes was doing really well. Her home stood, proudly at the end of a huge T junction. Yet she was not only doing well, she was quite evidently prospering.

So what did he have to say to that ?

In typical Yap Cheng Hai fashion such a challenge was easily answered. "*Look at her front door huh*" he told me. "*See how it is turned away from the junction ? And see the house is higher than the road ! So how can the road hurt the house. It is out of reach of the shar chi that seems to be pointing at it !*"

Thus did I start to begin to appreciate the small nuances of feng shui diagnosis. Of course, Yap Cheng Hai was always very dramatic. And over the course of several months he pointed out one example after another of structures that caused *shar chi.*

He termed these structures *secret arrows with poisonous breath,* and he vigorously warned me to always be on the lookout for them.
He also taught me how to really see whether these same arrows had been deflected by trees and other structures that blocked it, thereby protecting the houses that seemed to be hurt by them. He was in effect giving me lessons on diagnosing landscape feng shui and systematically feeding my subconscious mind with valuable tips that were to come in so useful years later when I began studying the subject in earnest.

I was to take him at his word, so that over time, I developed an acute awareness of the presence of secret poison arrows, and became aware of the killing breath ! Later, I was to discover more and more examples of these offensive structures, and yet I did not realize then that the main door of my very own home, then located in Kenny Hills was being directly hit by a huge and massively threatening poison arrow ! Truly a case of totally missing what is in effect right in front of one's very nose !

I was to realize, much later, that acute awareness of one's surroundings and one's environment is vital in the practice of feng shui. The study of this science must start with thoroughly understanding landscape feng shui ... in the process becoming aware of the nature of panorama and structures, and analyzing the flow of *chi* in order to be able to tell whether it was the good *sheng chi* or the bad malignant *shar chi* !

Green dragons and white tigers ...
Thus began for me an awakening to my surroundings, and my work space. Feng shui would bring me great success, Yap Cheng Hai told me, as well as wonderful adventures. Thus did he provide me with the carrot to keep on investigating ...

The first thing I learnt about feng shui was the sheer richness of symbolism associated with its practice. Everything in feng shui is described in terms of symbols, using mainly *dragon* metaphors.

I discovered and made friends with the *green dragon* of the East and the *white tiger* of the West ... and later I became acquainted with the *black turtle* of the North and the *crimson phoenix* of the South .... it did not take me long to realize that references to these celestial creatures was purely symbolic ... and that it is permissible, indeed sometimes necessary to stretch the point and actually imagine *seeing* dragons and tigers nestled amongst hills and trees, or cradled along city streets in the form of modern buildings.

And when they were missing, that it could be just as effective if we were to simulate their presence with pictures or sculptures of these symbols ...

Yap Cheng Hai told me there were specific guidelines decreed by feng shui which enabled those who knew how, to identify the locations of dragons and tigers in order that one's dwelling place may then be correctly aligned to tap the massive amounts of *sheng chi* released by the symbolic dragons and tigers !

Landscape feng shui ...
was actually very easy to learn, but practicing it was another matter altogether. I remember once asking a feng shui Master in Hong Kong, as he sailed in my boat upon the waters south of Hong Kong island during the early Eighties ... `` *just how do you recognize which hills are dragon hills and which are tigers ?*'' and he had merely smiled an indulgent smile before replying `` *it comes with experience* ''.

Not every feng shui expert is as willing, or as generous to part with their *kung fu* (ie their secret knowledge) as Yap Cheng Hai was !

The study of feng shui can sometimes be quite frustrating. Looking back in retrospect, I have to confess that while I was interested in the subject, I was neither a disciplined student nor was I ardently obsessed by it. I really only half believed Yap Cheng Hai's claims of feng shui potency, but I respected that here was something intrinsically Chinese which was also mysterious.

It also seemed to hold out a great promise, and who wouldn't want more luck in their lives ? It would have been dumb of me to brush aside such valuable expertise being given to me so freely !

I continued to be entertained by Yap Cheng Hai's narratives on the do's and don'ts of simple feng shui practice, and I tried not to be juvenile or pompous or patronizing about it. In fact I actually started making notes about it in my journal. This habit I have of recording all the bits and pieces of knowledge is something I have done ever since I can remember, and the startling gems that came out of my regular *kung fu* lessons was to be an unexpected source of valuable information in later years.

Feng Shui also provided the basis for me to forge a very powerful and close friendship with Yap Cheng Hai, whom by then I had come to regard as my *si fu* or teacher. His life had touched mine at a time when I was young and impressionable. He was so much older than me, yet we got along so well, to the extent that I often remarked to him that we must have lived together in some previous lifetime ... that my *karma* must somehow be intertwined with his.

I used to joke that probably one of the tasks of his present lifetime, must have been to point me in the right direction and help me satisfy the higher purpose of my *karma* in this lifetime. For of course, being a Buddhist, I believe in the cycle of births and rebirths; just as I also believe in the philosophy of *karma*.

Over the years Yap Cheng Hai was to open my eyes to a great deal of new knowledge about things I knew nothing about, and which he seemed to know a lot about. Thus did we become not just student and *si fu*, but also very close chums. It is probably this close friendship which created the *kum cheng* or goodwill that made him agree to let me have access to his feng shui formulas, and which enabled me to write three of my compass school formula feng shui books.

Back then in 1973, Yap Cheng Hai also became my personal feng shui consultant. When we built our own home, I asked him to check the feng shui for us, and it was then that we came face to face with my first *poison arrow*. I discovered that a huge tree in front of the main door of our old home was directing masses of *shar chi* at us, effectively blocking our family luck, and thus impairing our ability to have a baby.

I went to great pains to ensure our new house would have no problems of this kind. Feng shui became very important to me, and I believe it was then that I began to take it seriously. I started to investigate feng shui, and in the ensuing years, it was to become a journey of discovery that would unlock many of the living earth's prosperity secrets ...

BASIC FENG SHUI ILLUSTRATED
Examples of structures that represent poison arrows

The start of feng shui practice, according to Yap Cheng Hai, and other masters, begin with an awareness of one's surroundings, and becoming conscious of structures that represent poison arrows. These structures can inadvertently, and without you realizing it, be causing *shar chi*, the killing breath, to hit at your home, bringing inauspicious luck, grave misfortune and bad health.

Facing a T Junction !

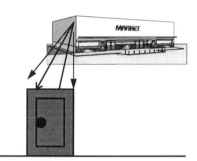

Facing the **sharp edge** of a building

Shar chi cause grave misfortunes, and are the source of much bad luck. They should be avoided, deflected or diffused at all costs, and a large part of feng shui practice involves knowing how to prevent shar chi from hitting at the home. But first it is important to know how to diagnose these offensive structures Illustrated here are some common examples of poison arrows. Notice they are usually sharp, straight and threatening. But their deadly arrows cause problems only when they are directly pointing at the home or the main door !

Triangular roof lines or those that appear pointed and hostile are the most common causes of poison arrows. These sharp edges send out masses *of shar chi* that can harm your feng shui.

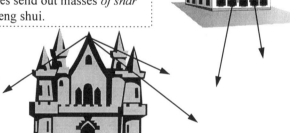

Examples of other structures to avoid facing directly are a **church steeple**, X **shaped crosses** of any sort as in a windmill, transmission **towers** or **tall factory chimneys**. These become the dreaded poison arrows of feng shui ...

MY PERSONAL FENG SHUI STORIES

CORPORATE CAREER YEARS
Good feng shui brings success on the career front
The wall gets built and I meet Quek
Corner office brings good feng shui
A bumper year of promotions

QUEK BUYS A BANK, AND I BECOME A BANKER
Landing smack in the middle of bank run
A different ball game and a different league
Using feng shui to protect the bank
The feng shui project
The redrawn dragon logo
The feng shui of the head office
My personal feng shui requires improvement
Hopewell Center defeats my Pa Kua

FINDING MY OWN GREEN DRAGON
Carolina Gardens on the peak
Excellent orientations throughout
Protective guardian lions
The dragon does not fail me

THE ACQUISITION OF DRAGON SEED
Where did I find the courage to make the bid
A series of brilliant coincidences
Did we really do it ?
Introducing feng shui into the store
A great new feeling
Building the Home and Design Center
Heiress … overconfidence and poor feng shui

CHAPTER THREE
CORPORATE CAREER YEARS
 ... Good feng shui brings success on the career front ..

In 1976, when I returned from the United States after completing my MBA, embarking on a corporate career became an important part of my life's aspirations. So Yap Cheng Hai's inputs about career feng shui became very important to me, especially the *success* part of feng shui practice. When he had originally designed the feng shui of our new house, having a baby had been our cardinal aspiration. Now I was to tell him that career luck was also important !

Our door directions and sleeping orientations had already been worked out so that my husband and I each had our own doors, and we were now sleeping with our heads pointed to <u>his</u> *sheng chi* direction. In addition we had also located the master bedroom in <u>his</u> *nien yen* corner. These two features would create favorable *descendants luck* for <u>him,</u> thereby enhancing <u>our</u> chances for getting a baby. But by then, my career had become important to me so I wanted Yap Cheng Hai to also improve my success potential with feng shui.

Frontage of land too large
For career success, Yap Cheng Hai intimated that two things had to be corrected. One was the shape of our land. The frontage of the land, he said, was too long relative to the back boundary. As such, he suggested that we should artificially reduce the size of the frontage by growing a row of Christmas trees to create a boundary that would in effect cut off part of the garden. I implemented this suggestion of his but as everyone knows trees take time to grow so he told us not to expect to feel the favorable effect of this correction immediately.

Part of garden cut off

Back boundary is narrower than front boundary. Trees correct this.

Years later after I had gone to live in Hong Kong and come back, I was to cut down those trees because feng shui masters there were not in complete agreement over the favorable or unfavorable effect of having a large frontage. At any rate by then I had become sufficiently knowledgeable about the subject, and I was confident that reclaiming this part of the garden by chopping down those trees would do little harm to us.

Direction of water flow wrong ...
The second matter brought up by Yap Cheng Hai was more serious. It concerned the direction of the water flow of the monsoon drain outside the house. This was most significant. The water was ostensibly flowing in the wrong direction. Instead of right to left, to suit the orientation of my front door, the drain outside was flowing from left to right in full view of my door.

So what shall I do I asked him.

You must build a solid wall in front to block out the drain completely, he said. *Make it a brick wall, so that from any angle the outside drain is not visible. You must do this as soon as possible if you want your career to take off !*

Yap Cheng Hai in those days had become something of an expert on water, and he often told me his knowledge of water feng shui was second to no one else in our part of the world. And since water was the vital feature to focus on if one wanted to be successful and rich, I knew that what he was telling me about the water was very significant. I could not wait to get the vital wall built. !

But fate has a hand in feng shui too because as it turned out, it took my husband exactly eighteen months to actually get down to making plans for the wall to be constructed.. In those days I left big things like that to him. That he did not see it as sufficiently important was to be one of the bones of contention between us.

Tough times on the career front
I was meanwhile having a really hard time getting started on a career. Finding a job in Kuala Lumpur turned out to be unexpectedly difficult. No one I approached was prepared to consider me at all. They dismissed me as being too highly qualified, and assumed that I must be exorbitantly expensive. Even the American companies which had hired me back there in the States had no interest in me in my home country.

Perhaps my feng shui really was not very propitious. After all I was sleeping in (for me at least) an unfavorable room of the house. My sleeping direction was all wrong. Of course they were excellent for my husband but they were bad for *me* ! And then of course I was also using *his* main door to get in and out of the house, because the door that was meant to be facing *my good direction* had been constructed as a heavy sliding door with a layer of grills. Opening and closing this second door proved too much of a hassle each morning so I never used *my* door at all.

Maybe that was why I was not having any luck on the job front !
And then of course the wall still hadn't been built and it did seem like it would never get built !

Any way finally I did find a job with a newly established merchant bank, Asiavest Merchant Bankers which was a joint venture between several prominent Malaysians and the Bancom group of the Philippines, but I hated the working environment there from the start. Since I did not have much choice I decided to bide my time. I felt very defeated, and so rejected, I wallowed in self pity !

I decided then that Malaysia did not want me at all, that there seemed to be no place for someone like me. My thoughts winged their way to America and there developed in the pit of my stomach, a yearning to go back there where I had been so wanted; where I had felt so alive with enthusiasm. I started making plans to go back to the United States.

But once again fate or was it feng shui was to change the course of my life. It sent me a great blessing. Six months after my return from Boston, or looked at another way, six months after moving into my new home, I discovered I was pregnant.

A baby at last !
Becoming pregnant revived all my old yearnings to be a mother. It changed everything ... my stupid job with Asiavest became completely unimportant. In fact it was just as well that I was having such a cushy job. I went to work at nine and came back at five each day. I had plenty of time to prepare for my baby, and oh yes, I was very very happy.

To think that I had completely given up hope of ever having a child ! My husband too was ecstatic and I believe the following few years were to become some of the happiest years of our marriage.

I remember telling Yap Cheng Hai the great news and of course as usual he gave all the credit to our good feng shui ! I could barely dispute his claim; nor did I want to. In any case I really didn't care what it was that had brought along this child that was growing inside of me.

The following year, I gave birth to our darling Jennifer, who when we look back at the old pictures was a rather plain looking baby but to us she was the most beautiful baby in the world ! I loved her from the moment I held her in my arms.

And because my husband was as thrilled, and possibly also very grateful he finally decided to build the wretched wall I had been nagging him about over the past twelve months.

I continued to work at Asiavest after Jennifer was born and they even sent me on a so called training program to the Bancom head office in Manila so I visited the Philippines, and also Hong Kong where they had some kind of affiliate finance company. There I was to meet Cynthia Picazo who years later was to become one of my dearest friend, and also my partner in the Dragon Seed acquisition.

Shortly after I returned to work after my maternity leave, I met Penny Chang who was working with the Hong Leong group. She had approached Asiavest to arrange financing lines for the small leasing company which Hong Leong had just set up and which she was managing. It was a most opportune meeting because she encouraged me to join her at Hong Leong and boost the ranks of women there..

And a brand new strategy ...
By that time I was also busy making plans to leave Asiavest. I had given up the idea of going to America. Instead I focused on the task of finding myself a meaningful job, and this time I was determined to succeed. I formulated my plan carefully. I sat down to identify five companies which I felt had the most potential of making it really big over the next ten years. I worked out my criteria carefully, and at the top of my requirements was that they should be Chinese run companies, because I felt these were the companies that would most appreciate my skills and my training. Hong Leong had been one of the companies on my list so when I met Penny, it was like a heaven sent opportunity of securing an introduction to the top man ....

Nothing like going direct to the dragon ...
if one had ambitions to ascend the dragon gates !

Ensuring good descendants luck through feng shui

Sleeping locations and directions feature strongly in feng shui that has to do with descendants luck. The Pa Kua Lo Shu method, which we used, works really well in assisting childless couples like us to have children.

We had arranged to locate the master bedroom in my husband's *nien yen* direction and also for him to sleep in his best *sheng chi* direction. Both these directions would be great for him, being East group directions, although these were my inauspicious directions. However since having a baby was the objective of our feng shui, his directions had to be energized. Six months of sleeping this way brought the desired result, and Jennifer was born the following year. The way we activated my husband's directions and sleeping orientation is shown in the sketch below. Note how the compass is placed in the center of the house to determine the various sectors and directions of the house.

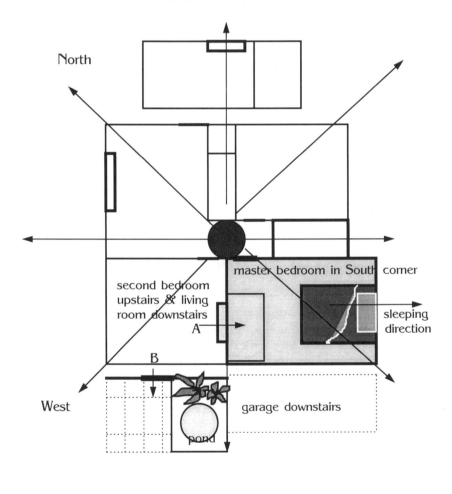

North

West

master bedroom in South corner

second bedroom upstairs & living room downstairs

A

B

sleeping direction

garage downstairs

pond

Making corrections to inauspicious feng shui

There were two major features which we had to correct:
1. The excessively long frontage caused by the shape of the land.
2. The direction of the water flow of the public drain outside the house.

1. PLANTING TREES TO CORRECT THE LONG FRONTAGE

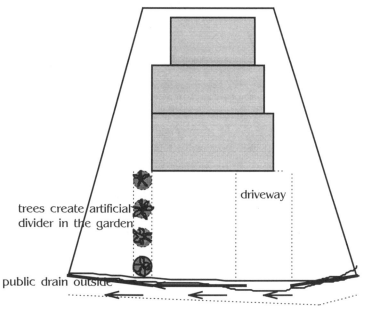

trees create artificial divider in the garden

driveway

public drain outside

2. WALL TO BLOCK OUT THE PUBLIC DRAIN

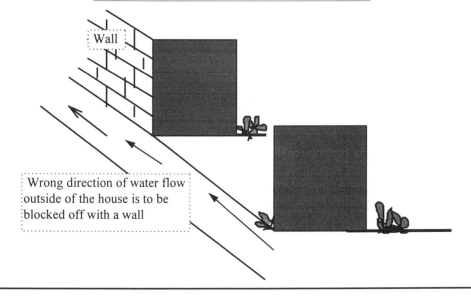

Wall

Wrong direction of water flow outside of the house is to be blocked off with a wall

The wall gets built and I meet Quek ...

There is a well contrived ambiance that subtly intimidates the visitor when you first enter (now Tan Sri) Quek Leng Chan's *domain* .... as befits the head of the wealthy Hong Leong Group, this tycoon occupied the entire floor of his head office building in downtown Kuala Lumpur. There are deceptively friendly looking bodyguards guarding the entrance, and the single receptionist who greets you appears lost in a sea of yellow carpet and wooden paneling. And there is a hushed stillness about the place...

When I first met him, I was stunned that this so called *China man* was so sophisticated. There is an aura of old world courtesy that surrounds Quek. He comes across diffident and refined, but also slightly aloof, all of which I was later to discover hid a basically shy personality. Quek does not give much away and his expression is almost always neutral. But I was charmed from the start, and unreservedly impressed. He was not just obviously clever, he was focused, very knowledgeable and very classy.

He offered me a job as his Group Internal Auditor cum Director of Industrial companies ! I remember that I was horrified because I had neither an accounting qualification, nor any sort of production engineering background

But I said, *Yes OK, I accept.* That was how I came to work for Quek and the Hong Leong Group.

I have always attributed my easy success to the wall that by now had got built in front of our house. By shutting out the wrong direction of water flow I had seemingly reversed my career and success luck. This did not mean however, that everything was going to be smooth sailing, but although the work was tough, I never felt so good about my career.

Corner office brings good feng shui ...

When I first joined the Group I was assigned a tiny room at the inner corner of the second top floor of the Building. It was a crowded busy office and the three plum rooms in the office were already occupied by senior officers already working there.

Though small however, the others had no way of knowing it had the best feng shui of all. Not only was its location diagonally opposite the office entrance door, it was also deep inside the office. There was a window behind where I sat, but a tall building located behind me compensated for it and symbolized the vital mountain support.

This would make me steady and solid in my approach to the job.

Most wonderful of all was the fact that I did not even need to do anything about my sitting direction. Indeed, as fate would have it, the location of the desk tapped directly into my best *sheng chi* direction. I started working for Hong Leong with a huge dose of confidence.

From the start Quek and I got on very well. I learnt a great deal about business from him, and I was to find out, as the years went by, that I learnt more working with Hong Leong than from the Harvard Business School. Which is probably why I am such a great believer in on ‑ the ‑ job experience.

It did not take long for me to establish a rhythm in my work, and because I was doing a systematic management audit of his companies, I got to know about the Group faster and more efficiently than anyone else in the company. The job gave me a strategic overview of Group operations, so that following his agenda was not difficult. By the following year I had been made Group Personnel Manager, and then (concurrently) Group Corporate Planning Manager, and sometime after that I got promoted and got appointed to the Board of some of his companies. It was heady stuff !

How marvelous it is to have good feng shui !

I loved working with Quek. Those were glory days for me and my career, and looking back, I marvel at my energy levels and the extent of my determination. I was working very closely with Quek in the corporate planning area. Thus we restructured the two public companies in the Group. Sovran Industries became Hong Leong Credit Berhad, and under it we placed all our finance subsidiaries. And Fancy Tile Works was transformed into the Group's Industrial Holding company, i.e. Hong Leong Industries Berhad. By then also, we already had the valuable Yamaha motorcycle franchise. This was actually my first major success for the Group, and it had happened within the first six months of my joining them. Talk about luck !

I had successfully negotiated with the Japanese and obtained the motorcycle franchise despite having to deal with the male chauvinists sent by the Japanese to find a new *partner* i.e. franchise holder for Malaysia. That was my first major negotiation on behalf of the Group, and I wanted desperately to succeed.

I remember swotting up on the entire motorcycle industry in Malaysia, and I looked around for all sorts of books which offered tips on negotiating with the Japanese (not many around those days) But most of all I recall making certain that each time the Japanese and I sat down to talk, *I was sitting facing my best sheng chi direction !*

That it worked quite spectacularly there was no doubt. Not only did I get the franchise, I even succeeded in making them waive the $10 million fee they had originally demanded at the start of the discussions.

Acquiring my Pa Kua shaped Intimidation Ring ...

During bonus time at the end of that year, Quek gave me a huge cash bonus, so big it represented more than a year's salary ! It was with that money that I bought my first *rock*, an 18 carat Colombian emerald, which I set in the shape of a <u>Pa Kua</u>, surrounded by rows and rows of little diamonds. The Pa Kua was a personal protective symbol. Green was also my auspicious color so I expected it to bring me enormous luck as well.

The emerald created such a sensation, later I was to name it my *intimidation ring* ! Because it never failed to intimidate everyone and anyone who saw it, especially bankers whom I approached to improve the terms of bank lines provided for the Group's business ! My choice of emerald had been inspired not by feng shui consideration, but because the heroine of my favorite book at that time of my life (Barbara Bradford Taylor's *A Woman of Substance*.) had collected emeralds ! But the Pa Kua shape of the setting was a feng shui inspiration which was later diagnosed to be very effective indeed.

The fight for Central Sugars

Flushed from the Yamaha success I then worked on the fight for control of the publicly listed Central Sugars, a plum acquisition which also owned one of the two cement companies in the country. This pitted Quek against his former best friend, (now Tan Sri) Khoo Kay Peng, the head of the MUI Group. I learnt an awful lot from that episode even though, as it turned out Quek lost to Khoo. It was the first time I was involved in such exciting acquisition work. It was such tremendous good fun, I encouraged my boss to let me handle all his corporate finance work after that.

I had also been successful at arranging the finance we needed to fund the acquisition, so despite his disappointment at losing the fight, he was quite happy to promote me to become Executive Director in charge of Group Corporate Planning. Less than a year later, much to my surprise, he again promoted me to become Managing Director of Malaysia Pacific Insurance (now Hong Leong Insurance). With the promotion came a brand new Mercedes 280, but also an entirely new industry.

What did I know about insurance ?

But Quek is like that. Just when you think you've got a handle on your job, he jolts you out of your complacency by giving you a totally new responsibility that requires you to learn your job all over again ! He throws you into the deep end and just leaves you to swim or sink. I loved the promotion, but I dreaded taking over Insurance. In retrospect I must confess I never truly mastered insurance expertise so it was most fortunate that while my calling card said MD of MPI, I was in reality continuing to do corporate finance work for the Group.

Unexpected Promotion requires me to move office.

With the promotion and the transfer also came the need to move office. I suppose it was timely then, because I was fast out growing my tiny corner room which had been so good for me. But I was wary about moving down to the tenth floor. The MD's office there was huge, having been previously occupied by the then MD whose departure from the Group to pursue his own business had created the vacancy that had led to my promotion. I also knew that office had bad feng shui, and I worried about it so much, I decided to bring my Yap Cheng Hai in to confirm the changes I felt were necessary.

We re arranged everything. I even changed the location of the door and bought in some new furniture. I was determined not to occupy a room with bad feng shui. Nay I wanted to continue creating great feng shui for myself.

It was on that occasion that Yap Cheng Hai introduced me to the concept of *feng shui dimensions*. He strongly advised me to have a new desk made, this time to feng shui measurements. I jumped at the suggestion and ordered a new desk immediately, one with custom dimensions. When the desk arrived I discovered it was too high for me, so I placed a platform under my chair !

And for good measure I placed a print of mountain scenery behind me to ensure continued support.

I loved my new room. It was more spacious and also more important looking than my old place, and with the feng shui properly done, I had little doubt my career would continue to flourish.

Meanwhile, soon after our corporate restructuring work, the share prices of our two transformed listed vehicles hit the roof, and Quek made a great deal of money for himself, as well as his family. It was very serious money indeed, and I believe it catapulted him into the corporate stratospheres, for with the capitalization of his companies enjoying such high price earning ratios, he was becoming a force to be reckoned with. It also provided him with the fighting fund to go after yet more acquisitions.

It had never occurred to me to punt on or invest in our own shares. Looking back I should have, for I would have made quite a fortune. That I did not was as much a function of my complete lack of time to devote to personal matters, as to my conviction that I would not then be sufficiently objective in my recommendations.

As it turned out, it was a good thing I did not, for later, Quek told me it was my indifference to the share market which had prompted him to trust me as much as he did with his corporate moves. I know that he is a man who plays his cards very close to his chest, revealing nothing of his plans or his intentions, even to his MDs. Yet I was privy to all or most of his schemes..

Thus I was the only one to know when he went after Hume Industries.

The acquisition of Hume

At the same time that he flew to Australia to close the deal with the Australian shareholders, I was meeting with the Foreign Investment Committee members here in Kuala Lumpur to get the unofficial stamp of approval for the acquisition. And when he returned with the contract in the bag, I was the one who once again arranged the funds to finance the acquisition.

I had met the Wardley chief Ewan Launder on one of my business trips to Hong Kong, and when we were scratching our heads on how we could package the financing, this gentleman sprang to mind. Wardley was the investment banking arm of the HongKong Bank.

I was confident our relationship with them was good and strong, and I had no doubts they would jump at the chance of arranging the money we needed. Ewan Launder directed me to his Singapore office, and it was through them that we finally arranged the money we needed.

I also approached the FL Smidth Group of Denmark to become our partners in the Hume acquisition, to provide us with the asbestos expertise and technology we would need. We had come to know this Group because they had been a significant minority shareholder of Manson Finance Trust plc, a publicly listed company in the UK, which we had successfully acquired earlier. I knew FL Smidth who were one of the largest Groups in Denmark, were looking to expand into SE Asia and I was right. They came in without much persuasion.

Hume was a stellar acquisition, and much of the credit must go to Quek. That he became aware of its availability was due to close contacts with some outstanding corporate people in Singapore, and one of them had tipped him off. That he succeeded in landing this plum acquisition can only go to show how fast the man decides and moves.

That I was lucky enough to work alongside him in the acquisition must be due to my great good fortune. I believe I must have successfully crossed the Dragon Gates, for shortly after the successful purchase of Hume, Quek made me a director of the company, and I spent several months doing post acquisition work, trying to merge the two corporate cultures.

Meanwhile, even as the Group worked at digesting the new acquisition, Quek was busy once more working on another corporate reorganization. He loved making changes to his organization ... this man. And he loves transferring people around. It is impossible to ever feel completely secure with him.

A bumper year of Promotions
Actually nothing quite prepared me for the great plans he had for me. I knew I was doing well in my career. Knew he liked my work and respected my judgments. But I guess I never quite believed he would actually put a woman to head any of his important holding companies. Into operating positions as general managers ... yes, but not as managing directors of holding companies. And certainly not as CEOs of publicly listed companies.

So when he asked me *Would you prefer to be Managing Director of Hume or of Credit,* I was truly quite stunned. Here he was offering to make me the CEO of a publicly listed company. It took my breath away.

That was towards the end of 1981, and in becoming MD of Credit (which I opted for in place of Hume because I preferred working in Finance), all the finance and insurance companies in the Group automatically came under me. There was some insignificant resistance at first but this soon fizzled out as it became clear to one and all that my promotion was for real. When the then GM of Hong Leong Finance put in her letter of resignation in protest at my appointment, she little realized it was not me she was challenging, but the boss. And of course there were dozens of managers within the company, just waiting to step into her shoes.

Those were heady days indeed ... but little did I realize there was more to come ... that just around the corner, yet further upward mobility for my career was in store for me ....

Because in another unexpected development later that year, during the Christmas vacation, one of Hong Kong's most aggressive deal makers .. Nigel Johnson Hill ... was to chase Quek halfway across the world, to sell him a little known bank in Hong Kong. Quek's coffers were full then which only served to whet his appetite for the really big deal. I was not to know then, that Quek's ambitions were about to take yet another quantum leap.

For of course Nigel succeeded. The deal made him a very rich man indeed (from his commission) but it was also to create enormous strides in my career, and massive changes to my life ... was it *earth luck* or my *heaven luck* at work ? Who knows really. Perhaps it was a combination of the *trinity of luck* ... perhaps it was even my *karma,* for the transfer to Hong Kong was to inexorably uncover vast new horizons for me ... it would considerably expand my visions, ... stretch my limits, ... and test my endurance quite beyond my imagination ....

CHAPTER FOUR
MOVING TO HONG KONG
Quek buys a bank and I become a banker ...

I had often been told by fortune tellers that after my thirty sixth birthday I would live abroad for ten years. Unlikely as this seemed I did move out of Malaysia to live in Hong Kong in August of 1982 when I was exactly 36 years old, and I did stay away for nearly ten years ! I was offered the job of Chief Executive of Grindlays Dao Heng Bank, Quek's new acquisition in the colony of Hong Kong. It happened   so fast I often wonder if it was all fated.

I remember getting a call from the Wardley boys in Singapore on the morning the deal was signed in Hong Kong. I knew the boss was in Hong Kong, but when the Wardley call came I could not tell them if the news they had just heard from the colony ... that Quek had bought Dao Heng ... was true or not. I did not know !

When I checked with Leng Hai, he too knew nothing. So I called Quek in Hong Kong, who was cheerfully celebrating the successful conclusion of the deal, and he sounded quite incoherent with happiness, and when he returned to Malaysia, we celebrated with champagne. All of us felt really high ...

Successfully buying the bank was a very significant and personally satisfying achievement for Quek. For years his uncle, the Hong Leong patriarch Kwek Hong P'ng had tried to get a bank license, but for some reason, his dream had never been realized. Now his nephew Quek Leng Chan had achieved what he could not accomplish. And so we celebrated, us ... the Malaysian arm of Hong Leong ...

But buying a bank is one thing, and managing it quite another. When the euphoria had settled, we got down to the serious business of managing the acquisition ... and because I was then heading the Group's financial arm, it was quite natural for me to become the principal liaison between all parties involved. Grindlays had agreed to keep the incumbent CEO in place at the bank until we appointed our own CEO.
So for several months I flew back and forth to Hong Kong interviewing potential candidates for the job, none of whom Quek seemed to like very much. In between these trips I got to know the Commissioner of Banking, and also our friendly financier, Ewan Launder quite well. So I invited them to visit us in Kuala Lumpur, an invitation they separately took up with enthusiasm.

I cannot remember if it was Colin or Ewan who first suggested to Quek that I should be the new CEO of Dao Heng Bank. At any rate both men lobbied strongly for me, and because they did have Quek's ear, I suppose their strong support for my appointment must have played a big part in his decision.

As for me, the idea of becoming the head of Hong Kong's seventh largest local bank was a heady prospect, and I found myself carried along a wave of enthusiasm ... it would represent a major career achievement.

By the time Quek finally came out with the suggestion that I go to Hong Kong to take up the appointment, I had worked myself into such a state of anticipation I don't think I even hesitated for a second. There was never any question of saying no, never any doubts in my mind.

It was funny really because when I told my husband, he actually did not take me seriously at all. He did not believe it was all happening. I invited him to come with me. To resign his job and come to Hong Kong to do something else there. I urged him to be adventurous ... but as it turned out, it was my *karma* to go and his *karma* to stay ...

I had thought that I would leave to take up the appointment sometime at the beginning of the following year i.e. in 1983, but as it turned out events moved too fast and I found myself being given three days notice to leave.

Word came from Hong Kong that Dao Heng bank was having a bank run. There were reports of queues of people lining to withdraw their deposits outside our Central District branch. We all panicked, and that was the first time I saw Quek momentarily lose his cool.

You have to go at once, he told me, as if I would know what to do !

For heavens sake I had never been a banker in my entire life, and I do believe that even the most experienced banker would not know exactly what to do to stem the tide of a bank run. But I figured that was not the time to remind him of this tiny little fact !

How bad is it ? I asked stupidly ... but it was a moot question really because however bad it was, we would have to move fast ... and so I flew to Hong Kong, to a new job, a new environment, and a huge crisis !

Landing smack in the middle of a bank run
Thus did I go through my first baptism of fire !

I am perhaps the only bank CEO I know who had to take up appointment in the middle of a bank run. For those of you readers who cannot appreciate how scary a bank run is, perhaps I should tell you that once it gathers momentum, a bank run totally destroys a bank, and if the tide of money flowing out is not quickly stemmed, even if the bank gets rescued, it takes years for it to recover. Because what happens is that the bank then runs out of cash and completely loses its liquidity ...

When I touched down in Hong Kong I went straight to the bank to find out exactly what had happened. The local managers informed me that the grapevine was already buzzing with talk that we were in trouble.

How bad is it, I asked.
Manageable, they told me, *but we must do something*
So what do you need done I asked them. I figured that at a time like that the best people to advise me were my own front-line managers, the people who had to actually deal with the situation.

Get us more cash, they said. *We need a lot of standby cash.*

So I made an urgent call to the Hong Kong Bank and was put through to their General Manager Peter Wrangham. He too had heard about the *run,* and was expecting a call from us. I introduced myself and asked if I could come over immediately. He said yes and I sped to his office which was within walking distance. Peter surely is the nicest type of solid dependable and very sharp banker. Without spending time on niceties the first question he asked me was *How much do you need ?*

I stared speechlessly at him, momentarily stunned at my stupidity for not having asked for the numbers before dashing out of the office !

(Gosh I had no idea ! What shall I do ? What shall I say ?)

I decided to be honest.

I'm sorry Mr Wrangham I cannot tell you. I've just got off the plane and I have not even seen the figures on withdrawals, so I have no idea how much money we need. I don't know how much to ask for...

In a stunning show of support, and without batting an eyelid Peter gave me the words that would forever make me indebted to him, *In that case, why don't we say a hundred million to start with, and if you need more give me a call.*

The stuff of dreams ? No just the Hong Kong Bank being the Hong Kong Bank ! Like a knight in shining armor, Peter had been both re assuring and kind. It was obvious he had summed up the picture pretty quickly and he had made a decision without the usual nonsense of having to consult people above and so forth. Peter had known it was a crisis and an emergency and had acted accordingly.

Later, when things returned to normal I decided to repay the Hong Kong Bank for their unqualified support when I needed them. I gave them Dao Heng Bank's clearing business.

A different ball game and a different league
I knew when Peter so speedily gave me the Hong Kong Bank's support that I was now operating in a different league. That it was now a different ball game.

Back at the office I called everyone, from my two friends Ewan Launder (*head of the influential Wardley)* and Colin Martin (the Commissioner of Banking) ... to important bankers and stockbrokers on our list. People I knew and people I did not know ... introducing myself, requesting for support and subtly reassuring them about our strength, our commitment and anything else that would create the relaxed impression that we were NOT a bank in trouble; yet doing it in a way which did not suggest for a minute there was anything that had prompted my call ...

I knew that the Hong Kong business and financial grapevine was all powerful. I realized that once it was known that someone senior from head office was in Hong Kong to take over the management of the Bank that things would settle down and we would be able to get out of the crisis, which, in fact we did.

By the following day things had started getting back to normal. But the unceremonious way I had been introduced to my new job was to forever make me super sensitive to deposit outflow.

I thus began my tenure at Dao Heng Bank more concerned about my Balance Sheet than about my Profit and Loss.

Which was just as well for the following eighteen months was to see the Hong Kong banking sector go through its worse crisis ever, with several spectacular bank collapses ... and even the *near* collapse of the Hong Kong currency itself caused by a one day *run* on the HK$.

Which is why up till today the HK$ is pegged to the US$. It was a very clever monetary solution to the politically inflamed uncertainties of the 1997 question !

Maggie Thatcher's visit to the colony and her much publicized negotiation of the British hand over of Hong Kong back to China had sent destabilizing ripples through the financial and commercial community. Everything went down. Property values, the stock market. retail sales, and most of all business and investor confidence ...

I was to witness and live through all of this even as I struggled to make my way up the learning curve of commercial banking. Nothing in my life before then really prepared me for that kind of frenzied but super sensitive scenario. I became acutely aware of the larger picture, becoming conscious of events that would affect me, and us, and yet were way beyond my control.

Nothing in business school quite prepares anyone for the kind of situation I found myself in, and I suppose it was then that I became much humbled by the way of the Universe. I developed a serious interest in things metaphysical.

> I started to really believe in the importance of *luck*, and I use this word *luck* because I cannot think of a more suitable word.

I was no longer living in a goldfish bowl, and I no longer had the comforting shade of the Hong Leong umbrella immediately available. I could not just depend on my expertise, or my management skill. I needed huge doses of *luck*, great good *luck* !

Many of these new perceptions were prompted by the fact that I was feeling the looming presence of the sleeping giant that was and is China. All through my time in Hong Kong I was to sense the shadowy presence of this giant awakening ... it was very disturbing indeed.

In retrospect I guess I must have just bumbled my way through, living from day to day, and coping as best I could. Because I was Malaysian, I suffered none of the fears of my Hong Kong friends.

So many of them sent their wives and families to far away places like Canada and Australia and America to get alternative passports, all fueled by their fear of an uncertain future in Hong Kong.

Getting to grips with the business of banking

At Dao Heng meanwhile, there were problems of bad loans. We had actually bought a good clean bank, but in the several months between buying the bank and my taking over at the helm, several large loans had been disbursed without proper credit evaluation or documentation.

I decided to impose an unofficial freeze on new loans apart from the safe mortgage loans that often make up the blue chip assets of most banks, and went after the bad ones with a vengeance. In the process of doing the latter, I discovered all sorts of clever fraudulent ways people think up to cheat banks.

One particularly interesting case I came across was when we recovered shipments of *rocks* which had been written in the LC documents as *jade.* I also discovered disbursements that had been approved by managers who no longer worked for the bank, and I found loans that had been made to people who would not normally have qualified. Altogether a classical bankers nightmare.

I realized then that in the initial months following the acquisition, even as we celebrated back home in Malaysia, unscrupulous white collar criminals within the bank itself had been taking advantage of the confusion that often accompanies an acquisition, to rip us off !

Meanwhile, as we started getting tough, I was to face another sort of dilemma. My branch manager received threats to back off on his collection demands and I myself received a bullet in the mail. Hey no one ever told me banking had such an ugly side ! Now I know why bank managers place security guards outside their homes.

Indeed, when I finally found a suitable apartment on the Peak (I lived in Hilton for six months), my concerns were so much on the security angle, I totally forgot about feng shui. As a result I ended up living in a veritable fortress, with three locks and heavy doors and a very sophisticated alarm system. When my daughter came to live with me, my elaborate measures to ensure her safety scared her so much, she stopped speaking for three months !

The social side of banking

Meanwhile, I had started making my rounds of all the other bankers in town, introduce myself so to speak, pay my respects, tell everyone about the Hong Leong Group and also ... attend the seemingly endless round of cocktail parties I was getting invited to ! This social side of my job was tedious and very tiring. I enjoyed visiting other bankers, but I disliked the cocktail parties ... and I sacked the overbearing PR firm which had been retained by the previous owners of the bank who nagged me daily about attending these parties ...

I was also to discover that the Hong Kong of the early Eighties was a very British, very colonial environment. When I decided to take over one of the LRC club memberships, The Ladies Recreation Club (which I was told was a very prestigious and expensive club) I actually had to be interviewed by nine (yes nine) ladies of the Committee.

Halfway through that particular ritual where I was asked the most ridiculous questions, (e.g. *now let us get it right ... is it you or your husband that's running the bank ?* ... humph !) I walked out and told them to stuff the membership. Later I sold all five of our LRC memberships. It was the same with the membership to the Hong Kong Club and the Jockey Club. Because I was a woman, they could not accept me as a member, so I shrugged my shoulders and decided that I would just have to live without those club memberships. I was never very much of a club person anyway.

Having grown up in a totally independent country where colonial dispositions and formalities were a distant memory of my father's days, I found the condescending (and chauvinistic) attitude of some of the *kuei lohs* seriously hard to stomach.

Which was probably one reason I never really understood why the Hong Kong people were not more positive about reverting back to Chinese rule. This is not a political statement, merely an observation of the differences that were immediately obvious to me at a personal level, between Hong Kong's environment and Malaysia's.

But I had no time to wallow in those matters. Indeed the main thing that concerned me in those days was the vulnerability of the bank itself, for, as the months went by, stories of financial scandals broke almost daily, and over the next two years screaming headlines were to be the order of the day ...

The Carrian scandal

Closest to home was the huge and massive scandal of the Carrian Group. This glamorous high flying company had been the darling of the Hong Kong stock market but with the collapse of the stock and property markets, cracks were appearing in the carefully crafted facade of Carrian.

It is just like Hong Kong of those days to have been so taken by the likes of George Tan, who encouraged everyone to speculate on the source of his seemingly great wealth ... some believed he was a front for the Marcoses of the Philippines. Others maintained he was actually a proxy for the Sultan of Brunei ... yet others speculated that he must have some fabulously rich Arab financing him ... as it turned out they were all wrong. George Tan had all along had access to the funds of Malaysia's Bank Bumiputra !

How and why he was given mammoth lines of credit by the bank was to become the *cause celebre'* of the Eighties. The Carrian scandal was grist for the financial gossip mill, and it even included a suicide (of a senior partner of the Group's audit firm) as well as a murder (of Bank Bumiputra's own auditor sent from Kuala Lumpur to investigate).

From my vantage point of Dao Heng Bank I followed the Carrian story closely because I was hearing disturbing rumblings from my banking floors. People, my managers told me, were talking about *Malaysian* owned banks ! People were saying that *Malaysian* owned banks were not safe. People were whispering it was better not to keep their money in *Malaysian* owned banks!

Using Feng Shui to protect the bank ?

At first I dismissed the talk as stupid gossip, but my Hong Kong managers are a very tenacious and determined bunch of people. One senior manager in particular was especially worried. Again and again he came up to see me and to alert me to the talk and the gossip. He had seen how vulnerable we had been when I had first come to Hong Kong. He did not want to have to cope with another bank run.

I told him not to worry. I told him we were strong and solid.

Hey listen, I said impatiently , *you know in Malaysia and Singapore, the Hong Leong Group is even bigger than Cheung Kong ! Why are you worrying ... and besides you know the way we manage our affairs here. There is no hanky panky in this bank !*

To his credit, the good man did not budge. He explained that while he did not doubt our strength and management resilience, what he was going to propose had nothing to do with things like that. Once again he urged me to do something.

Do what I asked him impatiently, *what do you expect me to do apart from making sure we stay conservative* ?

It was then that he sheepishly brought up the subject of *feng shui.* Speaking quickly so as not to lose my attention, he suggested that we protect ourselves with feng shui. He said he knew a number of feng shui Masters, and he told me that many of the officers in the bank felt the same and would I approve a budget for seeking feng shui advice ?

We had a very long chat that day, my Hong Kong born manager and I. It was a conversation that was to have   some influence over my life in later years although of course I was not to know it at that time. My managers revealed to me the reach and importance of feng shui to the business people of Hong Kong.

No one moved house or changed office without consulting the feng shui man, they said, and a lot of the good and bad performance of companies had feng shui explanations. Indeed even Hong Kong's bad period then had feng shui explanations, as did the collapse of the Carrian group. Leung told me it was due to the new flyover that had been built in front of their head office building, a flyover which resembled *crab claws,* with the building caught in its clutches !

I listened as they related many feng shui stories to me that day, and in the days following. I agreed with them, and thus he arranged for me to meet a series of feng shui practitioners, consultants and masters. I had insisted on talking to them before selecting someone to do the feng shui of the bank. Because I was already well versed in feng shui, I felt I would be able to assess the depth of their knowledge.

The Hong Kong feng shui masters were each knowledgeable in their particular brand of feng shui, but I did not feel right with any of them. From them however I obtained yet more stories, for each of course came with his own success stories and case histories. In fact, one of those who came was the father of one of my branch managers. They were very expensive. They quoted their fees on a per square feet basis, and charges varied according to the seniority of the managers.

I had by then decided that if I was serious about creating good feng shui for the bank, I would have to go through every department and check out the feng shui of every branch !

On the basis of their charges these Hong Kong *si fu's* were exorbitantly costly. I could not see myself being able to justify that sort of expense to my boss.

The feng shui project

So in the end I turned once again to my own *feng shui si fu*.
I knew Yap Cheng Hai would do it for me. I would pay for his trip to Hong Kong of course, but that was not difficult, and I would give him a reasonable red packet, but I knew he would happily go through every floor and every branch of my bank without counting the square feet involved. I knew he would not turn me down. I was not wrong, for Yap Cheng Hai responded to my call with great warmth and enthusiasm.

In all we devoted three solid days to the project.

I used the project to pay a visit to all 23 of my branches, so that I learnt a great deal about feng shui in those three days. We did a great many changes. We aligned sitting positions of managers according to their dates of birth, and we selected their offices according to compass directions, as well as to the *flying star* method which took account of auspicious and inauspicious sectors according to time considerations.

What surfaced in those three days for me personally was yet further evidence of the importance of feng shui. This was because those branches which had the best feng shui turned out to also be my most profitable branches while those branches that had severe feng shui problems also turned out to be the least profitable ! Needless to say, we soon corrected the feng shui of the less profitable branches.

There were also cases where newly appointed branch managers had caused branches to slide, and similarly others who had revitalized previously sleepy branches. Upon examination of their dates of birth and their sitting orientations we discovered the successful managers were sitting in their *auspicious* directions while the less impressive managers were sitting in their *killing* directions.

We saw examples of branches that were hit by poison arrows and flyovers that needed fixing.

The feng shui project achieved much in terms of improving staff morale at the bank. As to how much of it was psychological and how much the genuine working of good feng shui is a debatable point.

Nevertheless Dao Heng Bank never ever suffered from any more bank runs, and indeed the following year, despite difficult trading conditions, we even managed to improve our profits, and I also succeeded in getting the bank floated on the HK stock exchange.

Even when other banks started collapsing like dominoes later on ... Hang Lung Bank, Overseas Trust Bank, and Ka Wah Bank .... Dao Heng Bank kept going from strength to strength. Today, long after my departure from the scene, Dao Heng has successfully acquired and taken over two of these collapsed banks, Hang Lung and Overseas Trust Bank, and successfully revitalized and merged their operations !

Thinking back to those difficult banking days, I must confess that even with my strong belief in feng shui, I was always holding my breath. But it seems that the comprehensive feng shui that we created for the bank continues to work its special magic !

The redrawn dragon logo
It had been pointed out to me many times by feng shui experts that the Hong Leong dragon is an especially auspicious symbol for the Group. I have always loved the dragon logo, and each time we discussed whether to continue using it for the Group, I would always stubbornly vote in favor of retaining it

Not many people know the story behind this logo.

In the early days the Hong Leong dragon was quite different to the dragon of today. It has always been round of course but in those days it had been enclosed in a circle. I remember having been told that the circle curbed the growth of the Group, and that unless the circle was removed, it would be that much harder for the Group to grow. Thus we removed the circle thereby symbolically freeing the dragon.

I had also been advised to re draw the dragon because it looked ill fed and not prosperous enough. *Make it a fat happy dragon,* I was told.

And so I had commissioned an artist to redraw the dragon.

Make it look pregnant, I told the artist. That way the Group will have lots of new companies and lots of *children* ... and so we see the happy frolicking dragon of today !

Shortly after I arrived in Hong Kong, one of the things I had done was to incorporate the Hong Leong dragon into the Dao Heng Bank's logo. This I did by having the dragon clutch an auspicious Chinese coin with a square hole in the center !

I am not surprised therefore that in less than fifteen years, Dao Heng has more than tripled in size ... or that the Hong Leong Group itself has grown so much and continues to grow.

Less the reader misunderstand and go away with the impression that I am not giving sufficient credit to good management, I should point out that the way feng shui works is to create great good fortune during good times and ward off severe and crippling losses during bad times.

More than that, with good feng shui, companies will always be able to attract good managers, and the staff will generally work harmoniously thereby making the task of management much easier.

The feng shui of the head office
Much of the bank's good feng shui was due to the fact that we also successfully tapped the precious *chi* flows outside the head office. The building stands in Bonham Strand, which is at the end of Queens Road at the edge of the Central district.

There are five roads which converge in front of the building entrance.

Three of these roads approach the building at an incline such that the building itself stands lower than these approaching three roads. Because the traffic flow is slow, these features are extremely auspicious. This is because the roads are like rivers, bringing wealth and prosperity to the bank.

But to benefit even more from the confluence of roads, I was advised to place symbolic urns at the entrance of the bank which serve to capture the water as it flows down towards the building.

This symbolically captures the favorable and auspicious *chi,* and also allows it accumulate, and be captured for the bank.

Finally of course we placed the traditional guardian stone lions at the entrance as a symbol of protection for the bank. This would guard us from being taken for a ride by anyone unscrupulous ...

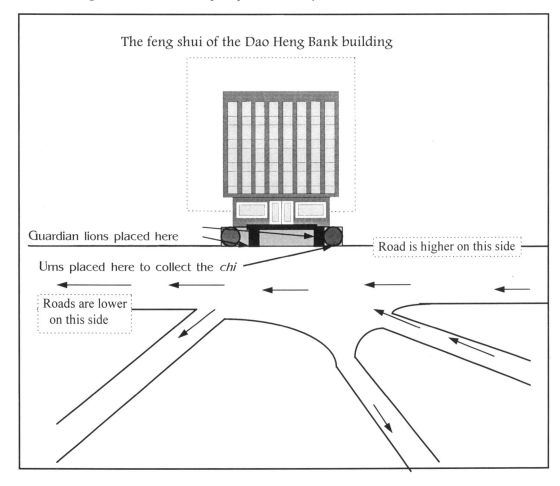

The feng shui of the Dao Heng Bank building

Guardian lions placed here

Road is higher on this side

Urns placed here to collect the *chi*

Roads are lower on this side

My personal feng shui requires improvement

Because my attention had been focused completely on the bank, I totally forgot to take care of my own personal feng shui, and even when my office and the bank's penthouse dining room were being renovated, I did not check on the feng shui. And when our Property people found me an apartment in Bowen Hill on the Peak, (after much searching because I was working to a tight budget) I become so sick of living in the Hilton, I gave them the go ahead without even looking at the place. My carelessness was foolish, and I was to suffer from extremely bad personal feng shui because of it.

About a year after I came to Hong Kong I fell desperately ill with fatigue and was admitted to hospital. I refused to call it a breakdown, and swore my doctor to secrecy.

The thought of the news getting out either to the staff or to the public scared me more than the breakdown itself. The thought of my illness affecting the bank's image gave me nightmares and I forced myself back to work three days later.

Only my secretaries Loretta Yuen and Amy Ho knew I had collapsed. Loretta discreetly made all the arrangements to have me cared for, and camouflaged my absence from the office. She even succeeded in keeping it from Mr. Quek, whose habit it was to call regularly to monitor developments at the bank.

But I remembered my illness at Harvard where, during my MBA days, I had been stricken with pleurisy in my second year and had only recovered after I corrected my sleeping direction ... and I knew I would have to immediately start checking on my directions.

It was then I discovered my sitting direction at work was all wrong, and so were my doors and entrances. What to do, the office had already been beautifully redecorated and I knew I hadn't a chance in the world of justifying the expense of redoing the office.

At any rate I also discovered to my horror that I had been sitting with my back to the sea and facing Victoria Peak. At that time I had had no idea of the topography of Hong Kong, and it was only after I questioned Loretta, that she opened the blinds of my office and showed me the mountain looming fearsome and deadly in front of the bank.

Behind me was Hong Kong harbor.

So how did I come to break the most cardinal of all feng shui rules which is to *have the mountain behind, and the water in front* ?

I wasted no time moving my desk so that I would capture the protective mountain behind me. But worse was to come for in correcting my own feng shui I suddenly realized that mine was an L shaped room (very inauspicious) and also, that by sitting with my back to the mountain I would get hit by the sharp edge of the corner which formed a deadly poison arrow ! No wonder my feng shui during the Hong Kong years was so bad !

My office at Dao Heng Bank was not auspicious !

This is what my Dao Heng bank office looked like. Aesthetically it was quite beautiful and impressive, with wooden paneling and nice carpets, but from a feng shui perspective, it had several very major flaws.

I had been sitting with my back to the sea and facing Victoria Peak, a most dangerous configuration, so that when I realized it, I lost no time in moving my desk. This is shown in the sketches below.

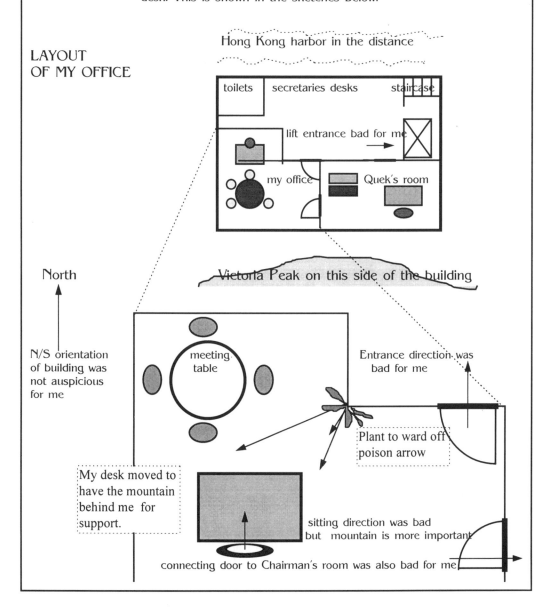

LAYOUT
OF MY OFFICE

Hong Kong harbor in the distance

toilets — secretaries desks — staircase

lift entrance bad for me

my office — Quek's room

North

Victoria Peak on this side of the building

N/S orientation of building was not auspicious for me

meeting table

Entrance direction was bad for me

Plant to ward off poison arrow

My desk moved to have the mountain behind me for support.

sitting direction was bad but mountain is more important

connecting door to Chairman's room was also bad for me

Hopewell Center defeats my Pa Kua

I resided on my own in a very large three bedroom apartment on the Peak of Hong Kong island. The apartment was spacious and airy and it had dazzling views of Hong Kong harbor majestically laid out in front of me. On a clear day I could even see the New Territories in the distance, and the hills beyond.

Bowen Hills was an exclusive address. It was nothing like the congested apartment blocks along Mid-levels that resembled urban redevelopment rather than luxurious residential apartments, and because it was discreetly tucked into the side of the hill, it enjoyed secluded privacy.

When it had been described to me thus, it sounded nice enough for me to take it without seeing it, which was a huge mistake. Because pleasant as it was, luxurious as it was, Bowen Hill apartments directly faced the gigantic Hopewell Center. I was to be told some time after I moved in, that this round tower block emanated bad feng shui to the buildings around it, especially if you were too close like I was. From my balcony, it seemed like I could just reach out and touch it ! It was said to resemble a giant joss stick, which gave off powerful *yin* energy that sent unbalancing *chi* shooting outwards !

When I realized this, I quickly arranged to install three Pa Kua mirrors to deflect the *shar chi* coming from it. I placed <u>three</u> Pa Kua mirrors, one on my balcony and one each above the two sets of bedroom windows facing it.

I had to do this several times *because the Pa Kuas kept falling off.* The energy coming from the tower block was too powerful for my puny little Pa Kuas, and nothing I did could effectively counter the forceful energy of the huge tower ! The situation reminded me of the Bruce Lee story, whose early demise has become part of Hong Kong feng shui folklore.

According to residents, Bruce Lee, whose name in Chinese meant *little dragon* had lived in Kowloon, the place of the *nine dragons.* He had apparently been told to move out of Kowloon in order to escape the wrath of the dragons, jealous at his use of their name. Undeterred he had installed a Pa Kua above his door (some say it was installed on a nearby tree) hoping this eight sided symbol could contain the dragons. But one autumn during a particularly bad typhoon (caused by fiery wind dragons), the Pa Kua had fallen off, leaving him without protection. Thus was he consumed by the nine dragons !

Since nothing could completely ward off the *shar chi* coming from the Hopewell Center, the only thing I could do was to block off the view. But although I did install heavy drape curtains, the marvelous lights of urban Hong Kong from my apartment often proved too irresistible to shut out.

I did make sure that I slept in my best direction, but I have to confess that, looking back to those days, my overall feng shui during my time at Bowen Hill must have been horrendously bad.

My marriage broke up, I constantly fell ill, my daughter could not stay there and finally moved back to Kuala Lumpur. I myself succumbed to the most appalling kind of ill fortune. I lost my protective Pa Kua emerald ring, and succumbed to various strange illnesses which caused me to lose so much weight, and to become so confused and self destructive, I landed once again in hospital ! This was to be the worst thing that happened to me during my Hong Kong years. I believe it caused me to resign from Hong Leong, because it was something I did for reasons I was never really clear about.

My decision to part company with Quek was made despite genuine efforts to retain me. I turned my back on him, and on my family and seemed bent on going my own way. Those were awful days indeed, and I believe I succeeded eventually in pulling out of that vortex of self destruction because at the subconscious levels, I was strongly resisting and fighting back; and also because Yap Cheng Hai reached out all the way from Kuala Lumpur to provide the spiritual remedies that were needed to eliminate the shroud of killing energies then affecting me. Yap Cheng Hai told me that someone or something had *bewitched* me !

But although Yap Cheng Hai succeeded in bringing me out of my stupor, he was unable to tell me *who* had been responsible, or *how* or *when* I had actually been *bewitched*. I myself had no idea.

It was years later, after I had returned to Malaysia and had got back with my husband again that I had a peculiar dream. I know this sounds spooky but it happened and I include this story here because anyone reading this should learn from it and take precautions against such things. In my dream, I felt a presence who told me that a woman I had once known, a woman who had once harmed me, and should not trust, would reappear in my life. She would come to my home, and she would come bringing biscuits, like she used to do each time she visited me at my flat in Hong Kong. In my dream, I was advised to throw the biscuits away. I woke up with this refrain in my head ... *to throw the biscuits away*.

I thought nothing more of it except that the weirdest part was that the very next day I received a call from an old friend (whose identity I cannot disclose except to say that she is extremely wealthy, and that she is not a Malaysian). I remembered her instantly, having seen quite a lot of her just prior to my resigning from Hong Leong. She had wanted very much to be my friend at that time. I never had reason to doubt her goodwill ! I had not seen her since the Hong Kong days after I left Hong Leong, and now she was making contact with me again. She said she wanted to see me, having read my books and so on, and so I said *OK come on over*. When she came, it was like deja vu, because she said, like she always did each time she had visited me previously, *Oh here are some special biscuits ... I hope you like them.*

In an instant I remembered my dream. I knew this time around, because my home in KL enjoys wonderful feng shui protection, I had been forewarned ... My hair stood up all the way down my spine, and I think that was when I knew ! I shudder at the memory of that day and I do not know how I did it, but something warned me to play it cool. So I did go out for lunch with her, but when I returned, I threw the biscuits into the rubbish bin *outside* the house. I have not seen her again since, and I hope I never will .... It was not Hopewell Center that caused me to fall prey to this dangerous and jealous woman.
It was my total lack of feng shui protection.
Here is a sketch from inside my apartment.. Note the poison arrows !

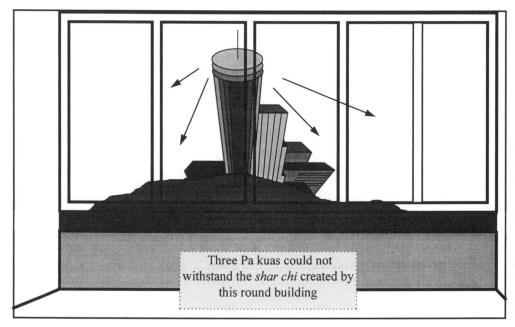

Three Pa kuas could not withstand the *shar chi* created by this round building

As to the motive that lay behind this woman's attempt to destroy me, who knows ? I can only speculate ... and there is really little to be gained from speculation.

But do I believe spells and these sorts of things ?

How can I not believe having once been a victim ! And especially living as I do in this part of the world where stories of *charms* and *magic spells* are legend. In Malaysia, Indonesia and Thailand, stories of *kong thau* a localized form of black magic are legend ! Can feng shui afford protection against this sort of thing ? I confess I do not know. But I do know that when you are hit by *shar chi* it considerably lowers your resistance, and the likelihood of you succumbing to those who would harm you, increases substantially.

Shortly after Yap Cheng Hai came to Hong Kong to help me overcome my illness, I moved out of my Bowen Hill apartment. At any rate after I resigned from Hong Leong, I had to. Those living quarters had been provided by them and having resigned, I had to move out when the lease expired.

So I went house hunting, and bought myself an apartment.

This time I chose very carefully ... My illness had shaken me badly, so that I would in future place my personal well being above other considerations. Henceforth I would use my knowledge of feng shui to protect myself first, and to benefit myself directly rather than focus exclusively on any company or business I was involved with !

CHAPTER FIVE
FINDING MY OWN GREEN DRAGON
Carolina Gardens on the Peak ...

Buying real estate in Hong Kong is the easiest thing in the world. It usually only takes one day to view, to commit, to arrange the financing and to buy ! Which is what happened to me. I knew exactly what I wanted, and I had been advised not to bargain. I was told that the few dollars I might perhaps save were in fact not worth saving since the risk of losing the deal altogether was usually quite high, especially with choice properties. Thus I was to commit and to have the papers drawn up immediately, as soon as I saw something I liked.

I was looking for something on the south side of the island; specifically I wanted to live in Repulse Bay, a location reputed to have the best feng shui in Hong Kong. But in those days it was not easy finding an apartment there. So when I was shown a reasonably large apartment in Carolina Gardens on the Peak, one that had a breathtaking view of undulating verdant hills and overlooked the Southern waters of the island, I did not hesitate. I bought it on the spot !

For I had seen, hidden in the hills below my apartment, the outline and form of a stunning *green dragon* ! I knew immediately that the place had good feng shui, and not just because of the *dragon* ... there was also a small stream which wound its way to the sea in the distance. It was quite spectacular ! There was also the added bonus of having both the entrance to the apartment block as well as the door into my apartment facing my most auspicious *sheng chi* directions.

I lost no time in sketching out the changes I wanted made to the place, and I managed to find myself a really efficient interior decorator who not only worked extremely fast but also did a great job interpreting my sketches. He understood everything I told him, being familiar with even the most eccentric stipulations of feng shui conscious clients. He even possessed a *feng shui ruler* so that all my new windows, doors and just about every cupboard and sideboard were designed according to auspicious feng shui dimensions.

I knew enough feng shui to be my own feng shui consultant. I knew I wanted a full length mirror in my dining room, to symbolize a doubling of food, said to be an auspicious feature. I knew I wanted a Pa Kua shaped dining table which would encourage good *chi* flows each time I sat down for a home cooked meal.

I knew I wanted my color scheme to be baby blue (reminiscent of *water* which was good for my ruling element). I also knew I wanted a large, spacious and regular shaped living room that would have an enormous picture window that opened out to the magnificent view. I had by then come to regard the dragon below as my own personal *dragon* and I wanted to be able to see it easily from the living room ... and finally I knew I wanted an enormous fish tank built into one wall of my living room to house the Arrowana fish I planned to put there !

The built in aquarium had to be very big, since Arrowanas grow very very fast. But the aquarium could not be *too* big in proportion to my living room. Balance was crucial. So to make sure it did not overwhelm the living room, I knocked down the dividing wall that separated the dining from the living room so that visually at least, a fairly large sized living area was then created.

I had also been told that to, represent auspicious good fortune, the Arrowana had to turn either *golden* or *pink* in colour, and its scales had to be shiny and to glow. The five specimens I had bought from the Mongkok market in Kowloon looked drab and gray. They were about six inches long, and their scales did not shine at all.

That would not do. I discussed the matter with a marine life expert I happened to meet one evening at a dinner party. He advised me to feed my Arrowana on a diet of live goldfish, *the more colorful the better* he said. That will make your Arrowana develop the most beautiful glow and shine ! So I arranged to feed my Arrowanas five packets of live goldfish each day. Not only did my Arrowana grow very fast they became exceedingly, exquisitely beautiful !

And they brought me enormous good fortune ! As well as plenty of money luck too. Much later after they had each grown to about sixteen inches in length and they each glowed pink with health, I was offered a small fortune for them.

But I never sold them. Instead I released them into the Stanley reservoir. Each of the fish swam round several times in front of me before swimming away to freedom. I had liberated them because I had also been told by a very old feng shui expert this was exactly the right thing to do if I wanted to follow through with even more good feng shui in later years ! I have included my Arrowana story in a later section of this book ... for those who might wish to try their hand at keeping this most auspicious feng shui fish !

❀ Author's note: The Arrowana is native to the tropical rivers of Malaysia, Borneo and Indonesia, where they are therefore easily available. Arrowanas must not be kept in pairs. They should always be kept either singly or in odd numbers. In Thailand, they have a similar looking fish but its tail is double ended, and this fish is also reputed to bring a great deal of good fortune.

Excellent orientations throughout

Because the apartment was large enough, and because I lived by myself it was not difficult to go all the way with the feng shui features and orientations I had to put in. Thus I pulled out all the stops in the renovation exercise. My bedroom was entirely restyled so that there were no protruding corners and no overhead beams. I also entirely remodeled the bathroom cum dressing area so that my bedroom would not be the inauspicious L shaped. I made sure my bed was of the correct dimension, and that I was sleeping with my head pointed in the correct direction.

Looking back I realize I must have been extra careful because of what had happened at Bowen Hill. I was determined to have good luck, and I did not want any mistakes to be made. So I did it all myself. I believed that because it was important to me, I would take the trouble to make sure I got it all correct; that I did not overlook anything, that I did not make any dumb mistakes.

There will be those reading this who might well get the impression that I was being quite obsessed about it all. I guess I was, but I was not taking any more chances. By then I had realized that my career moves of the recent past had been foolish; and that I had been careless to have allowed myself to get hurt by some stupid jealous woman.

Protective guardian lions

Finally I invested in two beautiful ceramic lions purchased directly from one of many porcelain factories located in the New Territories of Hong Kong. They were large, heavy and quite extraordinarily beautiful, and I arranged to have them permanently glued on at either side of my apartment's main door, but on the outside ! This symbolic placement of the guardian lions is very much part and parcel of defensive feng shui, and having seen them liberally used in the Forbidden City and also in Buddhist and Taoist temples everywhere where such temples get built, I came to the conclusion they must be *de rigeur*, i.e. that they were an absolutely necessary symbol of protection.

Protection against what ? Against people with bad intentions towards you, against petty thieves and burglars; and against *shar chi,* the killing breath that brings illness, misfortunes and dangers.

There is nothing spiritual or religious about these guardian lions. They are supposed to be some kind of mythical creatures and the Chinese use them because they symbolize protection. They are usually placed at the entrance of homes and buildings. They are not Gods or spiritual beings, and are never worshipped !

Later I was to find out that any kind of fierce looking animal can be used as home bodyguards ... leopards, panthers, eagles, even mild mannered animals like elephants ... take your pick !

In my present home in Malaysia, in addition to the ceramic Chinese lions, I also hang a painting of an aggressive looking eagle to guard my husband's front door, and another painting of a magnificent female African lion to guard my door.

It is vital that nothing fierce or aggressive are displayed or hung inside the home. This has the effect of turning the aggressive spirit inwards, thereby hurting the residents. In fact it is because of this danger that I never recommend the use of tigers, although some feng shui experts favor them.

This animal is one of the four celestial animals used in feng shui mythology, and one of the things feng shui experts warn against is that the tiger of the west must never inadvertently get energized in a way that turns its aggressive spirit at members of the household. Allowing this to happen results in illness and sometimes even death for residents.

Another variation of the warning about tigers is that those people born on years symbolized by small animals (e.g. rabbits, roosters, sheep, boar and so forth) must be extra careful when dealing with anything to do with the Tiger or Tiger spirit. To be safe, stay away from paintings or screens that depict the tiger. You can really get hurt if you don't especially if astrologically you are going through a bad period.

Having said this I cannot resist telling you there is one person in Malaysia who seems to have the Tiger well and truly under control, and that is our brilliant former Finance Minister, Tun Daim Zainuddin. I have never asked him if he was born in a Tiger year.

But I can tell you that his office is decorated with the most stunning tiger paintings ... not just one but several. Seeing those paintings told me a great deal about this man. For if anyone truly embodies the courageous spirit of the tiger, he does. And those tigers of his obviously have not hurt him in any way ...

I felt so good in my new apartment !
I felt safe and secure and very lucky indeed. It could all have been psychological as well, but why should I question the source of my feelings. I had not felt so good for a long time ...

Auspicious dates and moving in rituals

I also made certain that I moved house on a so called *auspicious day and time.* I selected the date from the Tong Shu, the Chinese Almanac and I observed all the *superstitious rituals* of moving house ... observing the time very carefully, boiling a large kettle of water and symbolically saying aloud *OK I have now officially moved in* ! And then proceeding to drink a cup of tea after that. Readers must take note that this observance of superstition has very little to do with feng shui.

It is instead part of my tradition and culture, and it has its roots in the Chinese astrological sciences that is based on the Ghanzhi system which describes god days for doing almost everything ... starting a business, washing your hair, starting work, moving house, moving office, starting construction, getting married ... I am not an expert in this science of good dates and bad dates ... but if you have access to the Almanac (which is freely available at any Chinese bookstore, except it is written in Chinese), it is quite easy to find out what the auspicious dates are !

The dragon does not fail me ...

I must have done something right because shortly after I moved into Carolina Gardens, something of great value fell into my lap.

This was a specially commissioned financial report on the DRAGON SEED DEPARTMENT STORES. Don't ask me how I got this report because it is not something I can tell you, but I did get it and it was a very good audit of this company, complete with past earnings, list of its real estate together with Valuation reports, as well as an industry outlook on the retailing business of Hong Kong. It was, by any standards, a first class report, and it contained more than enough information for anyone to make a decision on whether or not to purchase the company.

Obviously the existence of the report meant that the shareholders were serious about wanting to sell. There was even a list of all the shareholders complete with telephone numbers and addresses ! Talk about luck !

Few people were aware of Dragon Seed's availability. Fewer still realized the valuable piece of real estate owned by the company, especially the head office building on Queens Road Central, directly opposite the main Lane Crawford store.

When the report was first handed to me, I barely glanced at it, and so it lay unread by my bedside table for two weeks. And then one Saturday evening, I returned early from a particularly boring dinner party. The report caught my eye, so I started flicking through it ... casually at first but soon in great earnest. It took me three hours to fully digest the material before me, but by three a.m. that night I knew I had found my new career and my new business !

The recommendation of the report had been NOT TO BUY !

Whoever had prepared that report had been a most meticulous technician or accountant, but he or she obviously lacked experience of corporate strategy. Because my conclusions were just the opposite. I thought DRAGON SEED if I could get my hands on it would be a gem of a buy !

It was also brilliantly suitable for my state of mind at that particular point in time. I had already decided that I would package the acquisition of a medium sized company, something that was not very profitable which I could turn around, expand and then sell at a profit. Or I could get it listed and use it as a vehicle to acquire other companies if I had enough energy to keep going ... but I did not want to manage just any company. I wanted something that dealt in beautiful things ... either a chain of boutiques, or jewelry stores or better yet a whole department store chain.

DRAGON SEED was thus exquisitely suitable. Just the right thing for me !

It is impossible not to love shopping when you live in Hong Kong. There are millions of shops selling tons of magnificent products. Everything that is visually beautiful is available here. All you need is money ... or a genuine excuse to shop ... like if you owned a department store !

I had developed quite a passion for shopping, and the idea of owning and managing a department store was like the answer to a dream.

Besides, by then also, my buddy Cynthia and I had quite decided to go into business together so we had actually opened a small boutique selling silk clothes and accessories which we sourced from South Korea.

Cynthia Picazo and I become partners ...

Everyone should have a friend like Cynthia. She is not just clever and beautiful, but also warm hearted, generous to a fault and exceedingly nice to be with and to do things with - a true kindred spirit. She is neither pretentious, arrogant nor pompous, and I knew if I went into business with her, I would not only be more than assured of her honesty, for she is the most honorable of persons, I could also be one hundred percent confident she would never turn her back on me or betray me ...

I got to know her really well on a weekend trip we made to Seoul in South Korea. Both of us had excellent business contacts there. Cynthia also had a couple of quite spectacularly rich private banking clients. But it was not big business which had prompted us to make the trip. We were keen to discover the *back street boutiques* of *Itiawan* and when we got there, we found every kind of imitation brand name product freely displayed. The amazingly good quality of these *fabulous fakes* quite took our breath away.

But it was not the fakes we were after. It was the huge amount of gorgeous silk garments ... party dresses, cocktail ensembles, working suits, casual blouses we were looking for. We succeeded in talking our way into being shown hidden warehouses where stunning clothes were available for wholesale at equally stunning low prices. Cynthia and I (naively, I think) decided then and there to open a boutique. We went mad selecting the clothes for our new shop even though at that stage, the shop existed only in our minds. In all we bought about six hundred pieces of clothing over that weekend. In between we also bought about fifty or so imitation Louis Vuitton and Gucci suitcases, bags, wallets ... which we felt would make excellent gifts for friends and business associates.

Of course we were ridiculously overweight but that was not a problem because Cynthia knew the Chairman of Korean Airlines and he was more than happy to assign his assistant to proceed to the airport with us. In the end we did not have to pay anything for the extra cargo that went back with us to Hong Kong.

To this day therefore I have viewed the South Koreans as being amongst the most magnanimous people in the world ! Seated in our upgraded seats in the first class cabin we celebrated our new venture over several glasses of well chilled Dom Perignon. (I must confess I am very much a champagne person). It was just as well that we became so relaxed, and even a little high. It was to help us cope with what lay in store for us at Kai Tak airport a couple of hours later ! Between us we had thirteen pieces of luggage. We expected to sail confidently through Customs because we knew there was no duty on the clothes we had bought. We just never realized our other purchases would get us into trouble. Hong Kong Customs officials took great exception to our two *fake* Louis Vuitton suitcases as well as the contents of yet more counterfeit stuff inside. Oh dear !

We are detaining you, they said, *because you are trading in fakes.* They sternly questioned us ... did we know that this sort of offense was very serious ? Then only did we realize they were talking about brand piracy !

No we had protested, *those are not for resale, they are meant as presents*, but even to our naive minds, our actually honest tale sounded hollow indeed especially when we realized how much stuff we had actually purchased !

Fifty pieces of presents ? the Customs man remarked scornfully. And Cynthia, bless her dear heart actually brought out her Christmas shopping list and right on top of her list was the name of the Philippines Ambassador !

In case readers wonder at her list, I must add that the giving of gifts is a very strong Filipino tradition. They are always exchanging what they call *pasa lubong*, and I myself have received hundreds of *pasa lubongs* from Cynthia. They are always buying gifts for each other these Filipinos !

The Customs people confiscated our *presents, our incredible imitations*, but they allowed us to keep our silk garments ... vital stock for our new boutique ! That was quite an experience for us !

Undeterred by this dramatic start to our business venture, Cynthia and I nevertheless launched Je'Anne boutique (named after our daughters), our first venture six weeks later. It was against this background that I called Cynthia the Sunday after I had read the DRAGON SEED report to tell her I had found us our acquisition, and would she be free that morning to meet with me for an hour or so and I would tell her all about it ?

71

My apartment at Carolina Gardens

It faced the south side of Hong Kong island and had stunning views of verdant green hills that undulated gracefully into a valley where a small stream snaked its way leisurely to the sea in the distance. The air felt clean and smelled good, and nestled amongst the hills I could easily discern the shape and form of my own green dragon, quenching his thirst at the stream. I still have pictures of this dragon. The apartment was thus auspicious according to Landscape feng shui, But even according to Compass feng shui it was excellent for me because all the orientations and directions were stunningly correct !

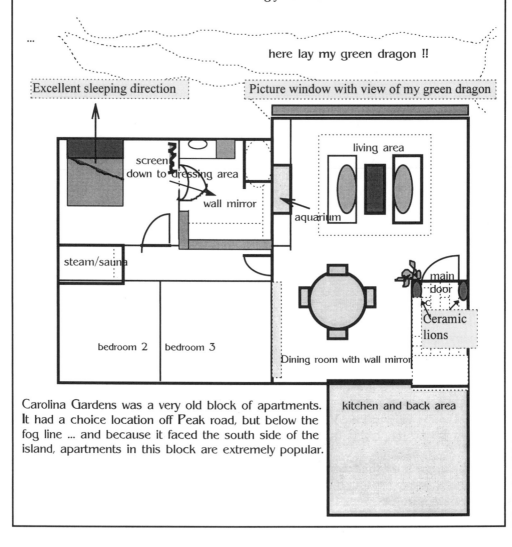

Carolina Gardens was a very old block of apartments. It had a choice location off Peak road, but below the fog line ... and because it faced the south side of the island, apartments in this block are extremely popular.

CHAPTER 6
THE ACQUISITION OF DRAGON SEED
Where did I find the courage to make the bid ?

In my more reflective moments, I often wonder if maybe I was always meant to one day own, for a brief moment of time, a piece of the Dragon's offspring, its *seed* ... because any which I way I look at it, the series of events which propelled me to make a bid for this department store chain seemed to occur so ingenuously, so smoothly, and yes, so naturally.

It happened very quickly, and to this day, I am astounded by my own audacity. That I went for it without seriously examining downside risks or considering the possibility of failure really rather surprises me. I still do not know from where I found the guts ... first, to borrow so much money, and then, to brazenly place it down on the table as non refundable *deposit* to accompany my audacious written offer to buy the company !

My offer to purchase was made <u>before</u> I had lined up the rest of the money, or had a chance to make a physical tour of the stores ! I depended exclusively on the report which had so fortuitously fallen into my possession.

I knew my twenty million dollar check would allow me to leap frog other potential bidders, if there were any. I also knew if I did not succeed in raising the rest of the consideration in time, (should they accept my bid) I would forfeit the deposit. There were also other factors that should have prompted me to wait .. for one thing, the timing. I made the offer in late November, giving the Vendors two weeks to accept.

They replied in the affirmative on the first of December but wanted completion by the end of the year. This meant I had exactly one month to package the money, seek out partners and financiers, arrange bank financing, undertake a due diligence and so forth ⁻ by any standards a very tall order.

I had completely overlooked that the month of December had less number of working days than any other month, especially in Hong Kong where expatriate bankers, lawyers, auditors, and venture capital people usually celebrated Christmas and New Year holidays by going away with their families ... and both Cynthia and I had ourselves made previous commitments, she to take her family back to Manila, and me to take Jennifer skiing in the French Alps.

Good feng shui all the way ...

I guess it must have been my extraordinarily good feng shui.

I had confidence in the *dragon* living in the hills in front of my home, and I had faith in my Arrowanas ... and perhaps if I were to indulge in a leap of credence and belief ... maybe I was also borrowing some of the courage and tenacity that are acknowledged as dragon traits. These are rather fanciful imaginings on my part. Yet it would seem as if I was being propelled by a spirit of unparalleled determination.

According to legend, the Chinese race was descended from this fantastic celestial creature. We think of the dragon as mythical, yet while I was researching for my book on the CHINESE DRAGON, I came across some well documented accounts of dragon sightings in China, some reported as recent as this century ...but I don't really care if the dragon is real ¯ for me he symbolizes great good fortune, so in my head, DRAGON SEED took on special connotations of good fortune.

What also struck me was that the company itself was founded in 1946 which is the year I was born. Even as I write this it sounds like I am stretching, and maybe I am, but as the events of acquisition unraveled, every stumbling block was overcome as soon as it was identified; and every negotiation proceeded smoothly.

We had no difficulty in convincing financiers and venture capitalists to back us, but we decided to go with the newly formed Prudential Asia, mainly because we wanted to latch on to their name. With Prudential as a subordinated financier, I knew we could convince any bank to lend us long term money at very attractive rates.

Pru Asia was a very cleverly conceived investment bank that married the skills and expertise of four of the colony's top financial brains with the gigantic financial clout of Prudential Assurance of the United States, reputedly the largest non bank financial institution in the world. I knew three of the four founders, Victor Fung a former professor of Harvard who later also became the Chairman of the Hong Kong Trade Development Council; Douglas Fergusson, whom I had met during his days as a corporate finance expert with Standard Chartered's investment banking arm; and · Michael Kwee, who was in charge of managing AIG's funds in Hong Kong ¯ all heavyweights in the commercial world of Hong Kong.

It was Douglas I knew best. On the weekend after I had read the DRAGON SEED report, Douglas had thrown a dinner party at his place to unofficially announce he was leaving Standard Chartered to do something else. What it was, he was not then at liberty to disclose.

But I had heard about the new Pru Asia deal through the grapevine so that when he asked me what I was up to, I said I was thinking of packaging a leveraged buyout of a family owned retailing chain that I thought had great potential, secretly hoping he and his new partners might be interested in launching their venture with me as their first client.

We parted company that evening agreeing to meet later in the week to see if perhaps we could work together on the acquisition. That took care of the investment banking side. Having worked in the area of acquisitions and financial packaging previously I knew we had to line up some sort of Establishment credentials if I were to succeed in fully leveraging my acquisition i.e. use borrowed funds to finance my plan all the way. The new Pru Asia setup with its *big names* was ideal ...

Next I had to line up auditors ... I was scheduled to meet with one of the partners at Peat Marwick on another matter, so I used the occasion to ask if he could get involved in a due diligence assignment ... and get it out like *yesterday* ? He said yes !

When I met Douglas two days later, he had Michael Kwee with him; As it turned out Michael was very well acquainted with Tony, the son of one of the founders of DRAGON SEED. Michael was mildly surprised that DRAGON SEED was for sale ... and when I told him I would pay $x million dollars for it, and that I was prepared to put a firm offer on the table, Michael, who is as sharp as a knife about these things, immediately concluded I must know something he did not ...

That was a great meeting because then and there, Michael decided on behalf of Pru Asia that they would come in on the deal as subordinated debenture holders. And he volunteered to deliver my offer to Tony !

We were on our way ....

A series of brilliant coincidences ...
With the promise of the Prudential name to make my bid respectable, I knew I would now need a lawyer. I wanted the best, and I have always regarded Tim Freshwater of Slaughter and May as the best.

Unfortunately he was no longer in Hong Kong, having returned to the London office. Luckily for me, as Cynthia and I were walking through Landmark some days after we had sent in our offer, we bumped into one of Tim's colleagues at Slaughters. Yes you guessed it; he agreed to take us on as clients !

Next Cynthia and I would have to borrow some more money to supplement our own meager resources, for us to put in as our capital in the deal. And we had to do this without having to pledge the DRAGON SEED shares since those shares would have to be earmarked as security for the big loan we needed to finance the rest of the purchase consideration.

Once again, I bumped into another friendly contact in the Landmark, and yes, once again you guessed it, that opportune meeting got us our loan. Perhaps I should explain. In those days, Landmark was the premier shopping complex on the island of Hong Kong; but it is also very central, and since everyone's office is located very near to this *landmark,* people walk in and out of it all the time. It is thus very easy to bump into people there.

By the end of that week, when Cynthia and I got together to review our position, we discovered we were still short of about twenty million. Prudential had agreed to come in with fifty million, and we were planning to arrange a term loan of about a hundred and twenty million. We figured we would need a total of about two hundred and thirty million or so to cover the purchase price as well as all the fees we would have to pay .... the auditors, the lawyers and Pru Asia themselves ...

None of our professional advisors came cheap. Quite rightly too. I have always maintained that when it comes to professional advice, *pay for the best and they end up paying for themselves ... pay peanuts and you get monkeys* ! As it turned out, we did in the end shell out nearly nine million dollars to PruAsia. Some of you who might gasp at this high figure should understand that without them, we would not have succeeded in our acquisition. We were really very lucky to have them on our side.

For it was also partly their name that enabled us to put the last twenty million into place. This came in the form of a phone call to Cynthia. It was Manny Panginilan from the First Pacific Group.

Manny and Cynthia had been classmates at Wharton, and they were also good friends. Manny had packaged one of the most spectacular deals in Hong Kong. He had got together a group of fellow Filipino professionals living outside the Philippines (those were the days of the Marcos era) and they had collectively convinced the mega rich Indonesian tycoon Liem Swee Liong to back them in their vision of building through acquisitions, a Hong Kong based conglomerate. Thus had been established the First Pacific Group.

By the time Manny called Cynthia to ask about the Dragon Seed deal, First Pacific had already successfully acquired Hagemeyer, the trading company which dealt in luxury products distributing Cartier perfumes and Christian Dior products ... Manny said he was interested and could we talk ?

But oh dear, their terms were difficult. We talked for days without coming to an agreement. Cynthia suggested we invite them over for dinner at my place. to try and persuade them to compromise. Manny and his deputy, I think it was Ric Pascua came to Carolina Gardens at around eleven. It was way past dinner time and we had almost given up on them. But I opened a bottle of red wine, and we sat by my window and I told them about my *green dragon* ... and we talked .... by the time they left, they had agreed to our terms and we had a deal !

Such then is the stuff of *dragon magic* !

By the following week, Tony, his relatives as well as the other eighty shareholders of DRAGON SEED had come back to us saying *Yes they accepted our offer*. So Douglas got his side going. He formally approached Standard Chartered Bank and Hong Kong Bank for the term loan. Both banks replied in the affirmative. We went with Standard Chartered Bank because they gave us a slightly better deal on the interest rate which was something like three eighths above HK interbank - attractive indeed.

By then, it was already nearing Christmas week. Both Cynthia and I wondered whether we should both go through with our respective holiday plans. And this is where we are such great partners.

We both agreed that above all things we should never lose sight of our priorities. So we opted to proceed with our plans. Our families were just as important, if not more so than our businesses.

Besides, we reasoned, almost everyone involved in the deal was going to be away anyway, so there did not seem much point in us canceling our holiday plans.

I also felt that with the series of coincidences that had propelled us thus far along in the deal, my dragon would look after things while we were away. So Cynthia went back to Manila, and I flew with Jennifer to Japan (having canceled Europe) for a week of Christmas skiing.

Did we really do it ?

Did we really go off in the middle of what was probably our biggest and most important deal ? Yes we did, and we gave ourselves a pat on the back for doing so. We got a letter from our lawyers chiding us, but by then we were on a roll, convinced nothing would stand in our way. And anyway he too went out of town with his family ... so what was he going on about ?

I returned to Hong Kong on the 27th, and Cynthia came back a day later. Completion was scheduled for the 30th December, and this story would not be so interesting without a last minute hitch. When we assembled the day before completion to check that we had finalized everything, good old Michael Kwee told us the Prudential money had not yet arrived from the States !

You see, money takes about three days to circle the globe, and for some reason the Hong Kong office's requisition must have gone in late. Cynthia and I hit the roof.

We were very conscious of the fact that by then, the Vendors were already half regretting their commitment to sell, that they had been approached by other suitors, and that we could well lose our deposit if we could not complete i.e. pay in time.

But Michael Kwee is also a miracle worker. I don't know how he did it, but by the next day, when we saw him early in the morning, he greeted us with a huge grin, and we knew that all was indeed well ...

The physical transaction of the sale ... all the signing and checking of forms and so forth took four hours. There were grandmothers and kids in that room that day, and some were in tears as they signed away their inheritance ... it was all very dramatic and sentimental ... but by New Year's day of 1987, Cynthia and I were firmly ensconced as the new owners and managers of DRAGON SEED.

Unexpected opposition from the staff

Except that, when we went to the store the day after the public holiday we were greeted by a sea of dumb struck faces, employees who had had no inkling the store was being sold. Tony had arranged to introduce us to them, but when he rose to speak, I saw that no one was listening. They were all staring at Cynthia and I. It was worse for her because she could not understand Cantonese. So she could only guess at what Tony was saying ... but she felt, perhaps more acutely than I did the tension and suppressed anger in the room that day ....

It did not take a fool to realize that the staff had had no inkling of the sale. Hearing about it for the first time, they did not welcome it. In fact they flagrantly resented it ! Many of them had spent a lifetime working for the company. Employed by the original founders, the sudden sellout by the heirs had implied total disregard for their years of dedicated and loyal service. They were angry, upset and felt betrayed, and who could blame them ?

In their resentment they reacted with uncharacteristic rebellion ... by late afternoon of that first day, the entire two hundred over employees of DRAGON SEED had handed in their letters of resignation to us !

What good is a department store without employees ?

And how do we cope with a situation over which we have no control. Their anger was not directed at us, only their frustration ... it seemed like a very childish and impulsive move on their part ... as if we could do anything about their predicament or their unhappiness ! Surely they must know that any gratuity or bonus for long service or loyalty or goodwill had to come from the previous owners and not from us ?

Perhaps they don't know, Cynthia said in a small voice.

I weighed that possibility. Cynthia was right. Perhaps they genuinely believed it was the new owners who had to take care of their grievances. And maybe we could turn this stupid crisis to our favour, use it to create a fresh start, to build a bridge of goodwill to a body of employees who had obviously been hurt by the what they perceived as callous disregard for their feelings.

Bingo ! The answer came to me in a flash.
We would accept their resignation with great regret.

We would acknowledge their hurt feelings, and then we would mend it by offering to re employ every single one of them. Offer them a new beginning so to speak. Invite them to share our vision, to work with us !

This way, they would become truly our employees, not merely inherited appendages that came with the physical assets we had bought. We would invite one and all to join the new management team that would take Dragon Seed to greater heights ... we would revitalize the company together, introduce new products, new strategies, new plans ... and put into place a new incentive scheme that would ensure everyone had a piece of the action if we succeeded ... the more I thought about it the more I got carried away by my own mental rhetoric ... it sounded good to my own ears, and I was confident it would sound good to them as well.

Cynthia was very happy to go along with me. *We'll call their bluff,* she said, for she did not believe they would so impulsively walk out of their jobs. She was convinced it was a temper tantrum; that most if not all would cool down by the following day. By offering to re employ them, we were giving them all a *face saving* device to back down...

OK lets leave it till tomorrow to react then.

That night I worried. That night I thought long and hard about the turn of events. Had I made a mistake ? Were there any skeletons in the cupboard? Perhaps I had been too impulsive. Surely I should have made a more thorough investigation of the company before plunging so recklessly into the venture ?

During that first day at the store, I had felt so much *yin* energy in the office and on the shop floors. There was a smell of lethargy, and of *chi* that had gone stale with neglect. The store looked and felt tired. And the faces of the staff had been listless. The underlying vibes were so full of negative energies.

I felt remorse creep over me. My euphoria and triumph at engineering the take over of Dragon Seed was now replaced by all kinds of doubts. The unprecedented mass resignation had shaken me more than I cared to admit. In front of Cynthia I had displayed my usual bravado, but inside I was quaking with genuine fear.

I slept badly that night. So I immersed my head in a basin of ice cold water when I awoke to clear my mind and rid it of any lingering fear.

Then I meditated for a full hour, desperately praying our strategy would work.

I decided that day to dress in red. Red was a color which always gave me strength. Having been born in the winter months of a *wood* year, I had diagnosed and observed that each time I wore red, the presence of the *fire* element would warm me and strengthen me.

Just like plants in winter need warmth to survive the bitter cold of winter. Besides, it being the beginning of January we were in the winter months, and I needed red more than ever !

Quite by coincidence, Cynthia too wore red that day. Which was wonderful actually. Two ladies in red was just what the feng shui doctor would have ordered to counter the massive amounts of *yin* energy that seemed to have accumulated at the tired store. Dragon Seed sorely needed *yang* energy. We needed to revitalize the sleepy passive dragon ! I decided in my head that we would be good for the store.

The first thing we did that second morning was to send out our offers of reemployment on exactly the same terms, to the staff. We would give them three days to decide. Those who wanted to ride with us were welcome to do so, and those who had no faith in us could leave !

As I said the red suit really gave me courage and strength !

I also decided to create a Personnel manager's job. And I gave the job to my former secretary, Loretta Yuen, someone I trusted and who, I knew would make a fabulous Manager. She had left Dao Heng to work at another bank, but she enthusiastically came over to us when I offered her the new position. My other secretary, Amy Ho had faithfully followed me to Dickson Concepts and was now looking after me at Dragon Seed.

I was so lucky to have both Amy and Loretta. They are such excellent girl Fridays, and everything else besides. When I told Amy what we had decided to do, she immediately got down to work, so that the letters were out by mid morning. And by the end of the day, every single member of the staff except for an old accountant who opted to retire,. had accepted our offer of re employment.

Glory days .... that evening, we opened a bottle of wine to celebrate. Now we truly were on our way.

Introducing feng shui into the store ...

almost instantly got everyone on my side. Dragon Seed's employees were hard-core believers of feng shui, and not a few of them were openly impressed by my knowledge of feng shui. Their impression of me had been of someone glamorous and very westernized, someone who had no business running a *Chinese* department store !

As soon as they knew about my belief in feng shui, and my knowledge of many things *Chinese*, it generated a new level of respect and rapport. When I started going through all the floor plans and began making notes of all the feng shui changes that needed to be done, it opened a floodgate of hidden knowledge.

There were many amongst my staff who had quite innovative ideas about what needed to be done. I was astounded at how much basic feng shui my floor managers and sales people and even humble clerks knew about the subject. To a man (and woman) they agreed we needed to get rid of slow moving stock, to make way for new stock, and we could do this by having a special Sale; then we needed a massive cleaning up job to give the shop floors a new look. A temporary but instant face lift !
And of course we had to increase the lighting, make the store interiors look brighter, happier, less tired ...

It was easy to identify the changes that could be made immediately. So I brought in better lighting, bought artificial plants to camouflage columns and pillars, hung windchimes at strategic places, installed large wall mirrors to expand missing corners and at cash registers to symbolize a doubling of turnover ...

On my furniture department floor, the black ceiling was immediately repainted in bright white colour. I had no idea why the ceiling had been painted black for it signified *a cloud over the shop floor*. No wonder the stunning leather sets and other modern Italian furniture were just NOT moving .... and we brought out beautiful crystal chandeliers and other modern lighting lying in storerooms as stock, as much to display them, as to serve a feng shui purpose. Nothing like lights to increase *yang* energy.

We then I arranged for music to be piped onto all the shop floors. I had read somewhere that music increased productivity, but I also knew that pleasant music attracts and expands the flow of sheng *chi* ...again, generating much needed *yang* energy into the stores.

A great new feeling at Dragon Seed

This became our *mission statement* ... to create, build and nurture a brand new attitude, inject some life into a sleepy department store which not only sold wonderful high quality stuff, but also had a great team of sales people whose latent talents had been lying untapped all theses years.

It did not take us long to get everyone involved and committed. And soon there really was a great new feeling at Dragon Seed, a positive attitude of <u>can do</u> ! In those early days, Cynthia and I were on a high that is tough to truly convey ... it was all very hard work, but the joy of being our own boss more than made up for the long hours and the *zillion* things that needed our attention. Along the way our new found friends within the company showed us the ropes and held our hands. Thus, weeks into the takeover I found myself flying to Milan, on my first buying trip. Products for the coming new fall season in August had to purchased.

By then it was the lunar new year, and instead of the usual celebration with family and friends, I found myself motoring miserably along the fog bound highways of Northern Italy in the company of professional middlemen who took me from one factory to the next, trying to second guess the fashion trends and colours of the next season. First it was menswear, and then it was ladies wear, and then it was shoes ....

The sudden shift from managing financial institutions to managing a department store hit me hard. Mentally, I had to struggle to come to terms with the reality of the massive adjustment I had engineered in my professional life. I have to confess I had no real appreciation of what the change would entail from an operational perspective, and it was while trudging between the showrooms of Dragon Seed's suppliers in Italy that its real impact punched itself into my consciousness. I do recall shivering with unease and disquietude.

But the die was cast. So I pushed my feelings of discomfort aside and got on with the job. There was too much at stake, and I had no intention of allowing any self doubts spoil our chances of success.

Cynthia and I had no specific agendas apart from transforming Dragon Seed into a huge commercial success, not just for us, but also for those who had placed their faith in us. Neither did we have a clear cut demarcation of duties between us. We had agreed from the start that there would be no rigid separation of responsibilities.

We kept our office and our jobs informal. We were determined to enjoy running our stores. And we wanted also to stay the best of pals. We would allow nothing (and nobody) to cut through the bond of trust between us. Instead we would give each other a moral boost each time the work got too much for either of us.

And I am pleased to say that despite the many difficulties and upheavals we, like all people in business, had to cope with, they never ever came close to creating distrust between us, so that apart from any financial rewards we ultimately reaped from the Dragon Seed venture, I believe one of the most beautiful thing that came out of that period of my life was our great friendship, which continues to today.

There are many complex trade-offs to consider in the management of department stores. But perhaps the toughest are the buying decisions. What to buy, and how much to buy, and in what mix of sizes and colours etc. .... There is a huge dose of luck involved in getting these decisions right. Buy correctly and you have a profitable season. Buy products that get ignored by customers and your bottom line suffers. Apart from merchandising and pricing and sales gimmicks et al, at the end of the day, the desirability of the products is what gives you a merely break-even year or an excellent year ! We appointed ourselves the chief buyers of the store because we wanted also to be able to follow through with proper presentation and merchandising. We split some of the departments between us, but in the important product lines we decided to go on buying trips together.

And it was on one of these trips, at the Frankfurt Home Products Fair that I mooted the idea of building a brand new store selling home products. Faced with the thousands of stunning products displayed at the Trade Fair, I felt confident that we could build a brand new outlet that would catch the excitement of Hong Kong's proud homeowners. Thus was born the concept for the Home and Design Center which took us all of six months to set up from conception of idea to grand opening !

Building the Home and Design Center
Revitalizing the sleepy stores of Dragon Seed had been a dreary exercise in refurbishment and rejuvenation of tired outlets. Starting a brand new store allowed our creativity free rein, and I set about the task with enthusiasm. To start off we searched for the right location and found twenty thousand square feet of space in the Central District that was absolutely perfect. I observed all the rules of feng shui ... the entrance opened to a beautiful lobby which allowed *chi* to circulate smoothly,

and settle before entering the store. Nothing pointed or sharp hit the entrance, and the entire floor area was a regular square shape that covered two floors. On the ground floor we located the table setting and crystal areas on one side and the soft furnishings on the other. In the middle of the store was a beautiful round staircase that wound its way gently to the basement floor which housed the home furniture, lights, and carpet departments.

I was eager to use feng shui because I wanted the Home Center to be profitable from day one. Thus apart from the standard planning, budgeting, designing and everything else that goes with the setting up of a new retail outlet, I decided to stack the cards completely in our favor by making certain the feng shui was not merely right but indeed, would be actively auspicious. I wanted to generate traffic and I wanted customers who entered our shop to actually make purchases, and not simply browse around.

We were extremely lucky that at exactly that time, we met Eliza Krohn, a brilliant interior decorator who was not just clever and creative and smart, but who was also efficient and honest. I can say that without her, our Home Center would never have opened in time for the arrival of the products we had ordered for the store, and we also would not have kept so brilliantly within budget. Eliza was completely in sympathy with my feng shui inputs. Mirrors were drawn in exactly the right places.

Aquariums were placed in precisely the correct corners. Color schemes were feng shui inspired and Eliza succeeded in muting colours and patterns so they did not look garishly obvious.

Most of all, she allowed the traffic flow of the store to meander, thereby encouraging the precious *chi* to enter, circulate and accumulate at all the right places i.e. where the cash registers were situated. I had been very particular about this because I knew that good auspicious *chi* never travels in a straight line, and that if it is allowed to gently meander, it gathers energy slowly, and therefore becomes more potent; and as it slows down, it creates pockets of *chi,* even as it moves.

This is a cardinal principle of feng shui, and it is for this reason that feng shui masters often advise retail shop owners to design their display cabinets, their tables, and their racks of clothes in a way which creates circular traffic flows. The best example of this sort of arrangement today can be seen in the highly successful Marks and Spencer stores throughout the UK.

In Hong Kong, one popular method of enhancing the day's taking is to place a full length wall mirror next to the cash register. This is supposed to double the turnover of the shop and is good for business. For our Home Center, I had mirrors lining the walls and shelves so that visually the store looked a lot larger than it actually was. All my cash registers were also strategically placed next to wall mirrors and I also made sure that nothing sharp was pointed at any of my cash registers. The effect of this sort of *poison arrows* can be very damaging to the profitability of any shop.

Another feng shui method I used was to tie three Chinese coins with red thread, and then paste them onto all our Sales Invoice books. This was supposed to have the effect of bringing auspicious luck to all my sales people since everytime they wrote up a sales voucher the customer would invariably want to buy something else as well. I had been given this tip by a practicing feng shui man who explained that the coins represented money and tying them with red thread actually activated the coins.

Our Home and Design center was profitable from the first month ! In addition to the good feng shui blending of elements and colours, I also chose an auspicious day to celebrate our official opening. (You have to check the Chinese Almanac to select auspicious days). We were also told that no one born in the year of the Monkey should be present, and it was because of this that Cynthia stayed away from the Opening. She was in Milan on a buying trip when the Home Center was officially launched.

We decided to have a noisy and loud opening. Thus we arranged for a hundred feet long dragon dance that made lots of noise. Making a lot of noise is supposed to awaken the *chi* and attract it to flow towards the shop. And of course to add a touch of glamour to the occasion we also hired Morgan Fairchild, the TV soap star to grace the event.

Most of all I believe that our new Dragon Seed logo also had something to do with the new shop's success. After taking over at the helm of the company, one of the first things I did was to redesign our logo. I hated the old logo which had a spindly looking dragon that appeared half dead from malnutrition. For the new logo we created a fat, happy frolicking dragon, curled into the shape of a crown to reflect the upmarket and luxurious products we sold, and to suggest some kind of royal appointment status !

I placed the dragon, drawn in silver, sitting on top of the words DRAGON SEED. The words were printed in purple. Together the silver and purple symbolized money ! Why ? Because silver in Cantonese was *ngan,* and purple in Cantonese was *chee.* Together the words *ngan chee* spelt money ! To this day I think of the Home Center with nostalgia. I loved the products we sold, and nothing gave me greater pleasure than to wander through the store taking in the beautiful things on display. Years later, long after I had retired, I often toyed with the idea of opening another Home Center in Kuala Lumpur, but by then, my energies were being channeled elsewhere ...

Flushed from the success of the Home Center, Cynthia and I decided to open another new outlet, this time a high fashion ladies boutique which would showcase all the stunning new designer labels we had signed up from Paris and Milan. Just as we had so successfully obtained exclusive names in home products ... ceramics, silver, crystal, porcelain et al for the Home Center, we had also been successful in discovering new brand names from the fashion capitals of Europe. We felt Hong Kong was ready for a genuinely up market ladies fashion store. Being admirers of the JOYCE chain of boutiques, we felt we could emulate her formula ... but in our enthusiasm, we made some grim mistakes ...

Heiress ... overconfidence and poor feng shui.
Probably the most serious blunder we made was in compromising on the location. In our eagerness to move fast, we broke the most important rule in retailing, and that was location location, and location.

It had proved difficult finding a suitable place in the Central district, especially one large enough. So we foolishly signed on the ground and basement floors of an oval shaped corner building that stood at the junction of Queens Road and Ice House street. This building had a reputation for poor feng shui. I myself had heard some of the gossip about businesses that had failed there. But I was mistakenly confident that whatever was wrong with the feng shui could be corrected ... maybe we did succeed in modifying the bad feng shui somewhat, but it was not enough, because Heiress was an uphill battle all the way. Stupidly also, we did not use the Dragon Seed name. Instead we used Heiress, and we gave it a different logo ... how foolish we were ! So despite all the hype, and all the noise level we managed to generate for the store, and despite its stunning facade and design, despite its racks and racks of beautiful clothes, and shoes, and accessories ... Heiress never came close to matching the success of the Home Center. I learnt a truly valuable lesson about retailing do's and don'ts from the experience of Heiress.

My beautiful DRAGON SEED logo

The logo shown here was my own
Dragon Seed logo. When I took over the
chairmanship of the store group in Hong
Kong, one of the first things I did was to
change its logo. We wanted something
which would revitalize the sleepy image
of the company which had such excellent
brand name products, and such acceptance
amongst the rich housewives of the colony.

We needed to desperately jazz up the image of the store.
The choice of the dragon was obvious, but what sort of dragon ?
Because we sold such up market products, we decided that we would require a
logo which suggested class and prestige, and what better way than to suggest a
crown ?

So we commissioned a happy frolicking dragon that would be curled in a way
that suggested a crown ! And to enhance its feng shui features we hit on a
sliver and purple color combination. This was because the literal translation of
the colours silver (*ngan*) and purple (*chee*) when put together would form the
words *ngan chee*, which actually meant <u>money</u> in Cantonese.
We thought it was rather clever actually ... but Dragon Seed stores did register
quite massive increases in sales soon after we launched the new logo !

Other feng shui features used in the store ...

included plants, windchimes, mirrors and coins on invoice books shown here.

INVOICE BOOK

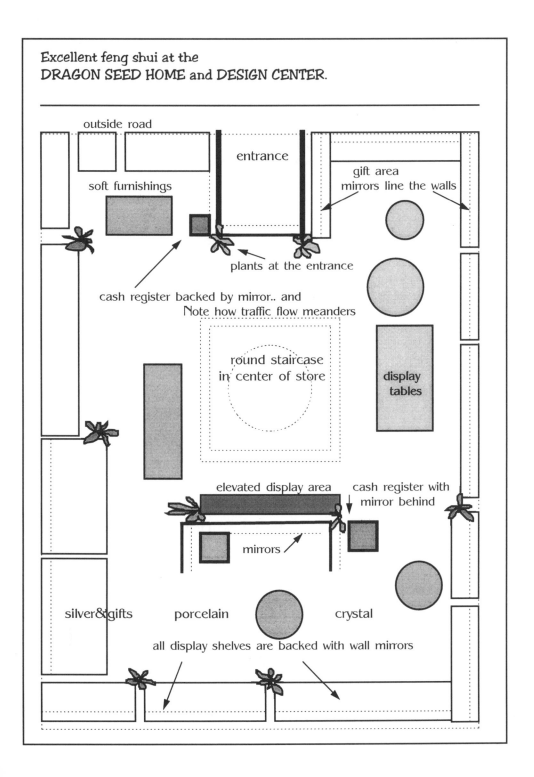

Excellent feng shui at the
DRAGON SEED HOME and DESIGN CENTER.

outside road

entrance

gift area
mirrors line the walls

soft furnishings

plants at the entrance

cash register backed by mirror.. and
Note how traffic flow meanders

round staircase
in center of store

display
tables

elevated display area

cash register with
mirror behind

mirrors

silver&gifts   porcelain   crystal

all display shelves are backed with wall mirrors

FENG SHUI STORIES FROM CHINA

CONTACTS WITH CHINA
Visits to the Middle Kingdom open new doorways
A meeting of minds with Harvard educated Dr. Fong
Bank of China invites me to visit China
The Great wall and the Ming Tombs

IMPERIAL FENG SHUI OF THE FORBIDDEN CITY
Feng shui features of the Palace Complex
The feng shui of the Empress Dowager Cixi
The living quarters of the emperor
Feng shui shapes and dimensions
Feng shui layout and orientation of the Forbidden City
Flow of water in the Forbidden City
Yin Yang balance in the Forbidden City
The five elements

FENG SHUI TALES FROM THE MIDDLE KINGDOM
How authentic are the ancient texts
The story of the first Ming emperor
The rise of Dr. Sunyat Sen
The feng shui of Mao Tze Tung
The funeral of Deng's father affects his feng shui

CHAPTER SEVEN
CONTACTS WITH CHINA
Visits to the Middle Kingdom open new doorways

Probably the most significant outcome of my years in the heavily *Chinese climate* of Hong Kong was the deep interest I developed in my Chinese roots, notably my passion for feng shui. I actively sought and pursued those who could enhance my knowledge, and one unexpected source were the wonderful *old style* bankers I met while I was running my bank; two in particular, from the Bank of China.

A meeting of minds with Harvard educated Dr. Fong

My first friend from the Bank was Dr. Fong. Shortly after my arrival in Hong Kong I had called on the Bank of China, to pay my respects and to introduce myself. In those days the bank was located in the old building and their brand new head office which today stands proud and high against the Hong Kong skyline had not yet been built.

I met their two most senior officials, Chen Haw, the genial CEO who reminded me of the laughing Buddha and Dr. Fong whose calling card described him as advisor and general manager. Dr. Fong and I *clicked* immediately. I warmed to him instantly. He spoke the most superb English, and was completely courteous and correct. He had a perpetual twinkle in his eye. Dr. Fong gave me valuable advice and played a big part in forging excellent relations between our two banks.

Dr. Fong must have been in his seventies. He seemed from a different world, a different generation. He told me he was from Shanghai, that he had been to Harvard where he had spent some happy years. I later discovered his life story contained clues of a romance of his era ... he had had to wait eighteen years to marry the woman he loved. That his life should touch mine so briefly must have been *karma*, for Dr. Fong was a learned scholar, and from him I was to pick up valuable inputs pertaining to the Chinese view of the Universe ...

I initiated overtures to make friends with him, and made it a point to lunch with him regularly. I found that exchanging notes with him, I could really learn so much. We talked about different things, about China's cultural history, the relevance of Taoism, and Confucianism in today's age, and in contemporary China. I felt very privileged. It was like having a highly qualified personal tutor.

Much of the insights he gave me aided me considerably in my deeper understanding and appreciation of feng shui. Dr. Fong's influence also kindled in me a raging interest in all aspects of the Chinese divinitive and metaphysical sciences. I was especially drawn to theories of *yin* and *yang* cosmology, and to the wisdom of the I Ching ...

It was the *I Ching* that engaged my attention the most.

Indeed, for awhile, the *I Ching* completely dominated my nights, as I lay in bed, trying to comprehend the translated words, trying to understand the symbolism locked in its stunningly simple sentences. Over time I came to marvel at the intense wisdom and philosophy of this great classic. I also discovered that in grasping the subtleties of the I Ching's meanings and judgments, feng shui fundamentals took on greater depth, and became exceedingly clear, and also acutely logical.

Bank of China invites me to visit China

Dr. Fong arranged for the Bank of China to officially invite me to join a tour of Southern China for selected bankers. The tour would include visits to the cities of Kunming in Yunnan province, the legendary Kweilin with its scenic Lijiang river, and the bustling metropolis of Guanzhou, which had been built, Dr. Fong informed me, according to strict feng shui principles. It would be my first visit to China, and I was apprehensive. In those days few Malaysians were allowed to visit China, and I had no idea what to expect ...

Being a third generation overseas Chinese in Malaysia and being completely English educated I had no special sentiments towards China. My parents had never spoken of China. We had long ago lost touch with relatives there, so that to all intents and purposes, China truly was foreign ... and yet, the trip must have stirred long buried and subconscious emotions for I was breathless with excitement !

Our party to China comprised the Hong Kong heads of Mitsubishi Bank and the Bank of Tokyo; Banque de L'indochine; the ANZ Bank; Security Pacific Bank; the Chase Manhattan Bank and the Urban International Bank. The representative from the Bank of China who accompanied us on the trip was T.Y Wang, then a very low profile, and seemingly humble manager at the Hong Kong office. T.Y. must in reality, have been a far more important personage at the Bank than we all realized, for a year later he was transferred back to Beijing, where within eighteen months he had become the President, and soon after the Chairman of the Bank of China !

Those of us who went on that banking tour with T.Y. came to develop a great deal of respect for this soft spoken and very understated person. We liked him a lot !

But the trip itself was a major disappointment for me. I was depressed by everything I saw. In that year, 1982, there were few cars in China, only bicycles, seemingly millions of them !

There were also few paved roads, only muddy streets.
I was appalled at the backwardness of the country. I saw antediluvian implements being used, and there was quite a lot of poverty as well. And there was little color. Everyone was dressed either in blues or blacks or gray, and that too a dull version of these shades. We passed quarries where men extracted stone, with hand held *changkuls*, and we passed rice fields devoid of any farm machinery. The food we were served was often cold and unappetizing. It was like traveling back in time to a more primitive era. Yes of course the scenery of Kweilin was beautiful but not more so than a great many other countries .... truly, on that first visit, I reeled from the reality of China !

One evening I remarked to T.Y., *So what's so great about communism then ... I can't believe how backward China is !*

He shook his head, *Yes it is not impressive. It is even bad ...* and then as if speaking to himself *but it was good when the communists first took over, in the late forties. It was good then,* he repeated almost to himself.

So what went wrong ? I asked

Many things went wrong he replied, although he did not elaborate. He shook his head, torn, I believe between wanting to explain, yet feeling that it was perhaps unwise to reveal too much of his own perceptions.

One of those in our party was a Vietnamese Chinese woman, Amy Sakkaf who now lived in Hong Kong with her banker husband Mustapha Sakkaf. Amy had a brother living in Guanzhou. He and his wife, both doctors, he a surgeon, and she an eye specialist trained in France, had returned to China in a surge of patriotism during the early 1950s.

Amy had not seen her brother since then. She wanted desperately to find him, and somehow, T.Y. performed a small miracle by locating him, so that on the night before we left Guanzhou, shortly after dinner, we met him.

He walked through the doorway of the restaurant, a wraith of a man, thin, diffident and quite stooped. He wore a drab blue jacket and trousers, and he looked years older than his fifty ought years. I swallowed the lump which welled up in my throat as I watched this unlikely reunion unfold before me. Amy opened her arms and burst into tears, and as they hugged, I felt the sadness of this man's wasted life ...

Later Amy told us her sister in law had been ill through over work; she used to have as many as sixty operations a day, she said; ... Amy's brother never forgave himself for returning to China. Most horrific of all, they had lost their daughters to the Cultural revolution. At first the girls had become Red Guards, but later they had been sent to the fields for rehabilitation and re education ... two of the girls had succumbed to the almost labor camp conditions. The family had lived on three bags of sugar and one bag of rice given them each month by the State... it was not a pretty story and I think we all felt for Amy.

Later I asked T.Y. to tell me about the period of the Cultural Revolution, the Seventies, but he had shaken his head gently. *Perhaps that was for us a time of madness* ... But he had been lucky. *I had already been posted to Hong Kong then, so I escaped it all,* he explained. Months later, at the farewell dinner I threw for him just before his transfer back to Beijing, he told me he had been in the colony for eighteen years.

In Guanzhou, arrangements were also made for me to meet with a lecturer from some Academy or other. Mr. Wang who shared a surname with T.Y. was supposedly an authority on the Chinese classics and was also well versed in feng shui. I had requested to meet with someone like him, someone who could speak English, or at least the Cantonese dialect, whose brain I could pick on matters to do with the theoretical basis of feng shui. I had a pleasant afternoon with Mr. Wang whose English was coherent enough for us to communicate with each other, but I was so distracted because he was bent backwards. His back had apparently been broken during the cultural revolution when he had been severely beaten ! Really, China sometimes is too much to bear ... I never saw Mr. Wang again but my discussion with him did yield some background of the old city of Guanxhou ...

We returned to Hong Kong from Guanzhou by train. There were no compartments on the train, just rows of PVC benches which were not comfortable. Somewhere along the journey, I pricked my finger and blood oozed out.

It was a tiny sliver of a cut but I remember T.Y. immediately taking out his finger to show me he too had a cut. And then he had put our two fingers together, mingling the tiny drop of blood and said *there, now we are blood brothers.*

It was a long time ago of course, and maybe he has even forgotten the incident, but I have not. Because I liked T.Y. very much, and knew I could learn much from him , not just about banking but also about the modern history of China. He urged me to study Mandarin, but my attempts were to be unsuccessful. I had no idea of course that he would one day become so important, or play so crucial a role in the economic opening up of China.

When he went back to China, he invited me and my Bank to visit Beijing. By then he had become President of the Bank; so we took him up on his offer, and accompanied by Frank Tung and Kwek Leng Sun two of my fellow directors at Dao Heng we flew to Beijing to establish correspondent banking relations with the Bank of China.

In the mid Eighties I visited Beijing again, this time at the invitation of Arab Banking Corporation (ABC) to attend the Euromoney Conference. ABC chartered a plane to fly their Hong Kong guests to the conference, and we stayed at the Great Wall Hotel, then a brand new five star chrome and glass hotel which looked out of place among the old buildings of the capital. Probably all of SE Asia's Chinese tycoons must have attended that conference and I have a three feet long picture of all participants as a souvenir of that historic occasion.

My China visits open doors to greater feng shui knowledge
My travels to China during those years of the Eighties, had an important fringe benefit, in that I could take advantage of my being there to personally view monumental feng shui at work. Many of these side trips had me playing tourist. There were also times when I was fortunate enough to be accompanied by experts who were well versed in the artistic, cultural, architectural or symbolic history of the buildings ... as a result of which much of what I myself had read came to life for me.

I was told folk stories of feng shui and other portents of greatness of China's leaders, from Dr. Sun at the turn of the century to Mao and Deng, and I began to appreciate the significance of *symbolism* to the Chinese. These and other stories of China's imperial emperors told me a great deal about ancestral feng shui ... and I have included some of these narratives, in a later section, as part of this collection of stories.

The Great Wall and the Ming Tombs

I spent a whole day motoring to the Great Wall, and to the Ming Tombs. It was a journey peppered with setbacks and unexpected stops. First the van we were traveling in had a burst tire. Then it ran out of fuel leaving us stranded. I should have read these as a signs to turn back, because when we reached the Wall I was consumed by an overpowering melancholia. I sensed a deep sadness there, a wailing kind of sadness, and it was not just from the biting cold which seeped through my fur coat and into my bones. Perhaps, it being winter, there must also have been a surfeit of *yin* energy which compounded my feelings of depression. But later I found a book which described the construction of China's Great Wall and it contained bitterly tragic stories of the thousands who died building it. According to history, every family had to send a male who would work until he died there. Husbands or sons sent to work at the Wall never returned, and when they died, the family had to send another male to replace the one that died. China's history is so full of tragedy ...

On the way back to Beijing, the bus was also scheduled to visit the Ming Tombs, another major tourist attraction. I had been told to go see the excellent feng shui orientation of the tombs. It was supposed to be classical feng shui. But I saw neither the Green dragon mountains nor the White Tiger hills ... but the drive into the site where excavations had been made, and where visitors could take an elevator down the shaft into the tomb itself was lined with stone animals ostensibly placed there to guard the tomb. I saw lions and tigers, and huge kneeling elephants.

When we reached the tombs, I descended into the dark, dank cavern and regretted it instantly. The Ming tombs were unimpressive ! When we came back up again, I saw yellowing pictures of excavated remains of the emperors. The pictures were caked with dirt, and were gruesome.

When I got back to the hotel, I worked extra hard at washing off the remains of the day ... I felt very bad. I should mention that my dark period in Hong Kong, when much bad luck befell me followed my visit to the Ming tombs. Call it superstition, but I will never visit tombs again ! The *yin* energy sticks ... and it could not have been good feng shui.

But in China I also spent a great deal of time visiting the Forbidden City, and it was here, in the grand and imposing Palace complex that much of feng shui came alive for me .... Here that I saw all the evidence of imperial feng shui at work ... !

CHAPTER EIGHT
IMPERIAL FENG SHUI OF THE FORBIDDEN CITY
Feng shui features of the Palace complex

On one of my visits to Beijing, I hosted a dinner for representatives of the Bank of China. We were playing host in reciprocation for their hospitality, and it was an interesting evening. Halfway through dinner I brought up the subject of feng shui and described my visits, earlier in the day, to the Wall and the Ming tombs. I told them I had not been successful at fully appreciating the feng shui of the imperial tombs.

The men from the Bank of China were most helpful. *If feng shui is what you are interested in*, they responded, it is the Palace you must see ... *perhaps when you visit the Forbidden City tomorrow we can arrange for you to be accompanied by someone from the Palace Museum.*

I gladly accepted their kind offer. And the following day, true to their promise, there was a gentleman from the Museum waiting for me at the South gate entrance to the Forbidden City.

He turned out to be my most valuable introduction, in terms of my quest for knowledge. For he was to explain many of the feng shui features of the Ming and Ching palaces that made up this huge palace complex.

Generally referred to as the Forbidden City, and located in the heart of Beijing just south of Tian An Men square, magnificent scenes of this complex were shown to the world in the Bertolucci movie *The Last Emperor* ! Built in the 1420s by the third Ming dynasty emperor, and progressively renovated by the later Ching emperors, many of the palaces, pavilions, gates and halls of this complex remain beautifully intact, and in fact have been remarkably well preserved. And because it is a distillation of many centuries of traditional Chinese palace construction, it is almost a perfect showcase not only of the arts and techniques of Chinese architecture, but also a splendid monument of the practice of feng shui at the highest imperial levels.

It took me an entire day to slowly walk through the City with Mr. Zheng, my guide who was a researcher in traditional Chinese architecture attached to the Palace museum.

I was lucky in that I was also provided with a translator who was most efficient in adding his two cents worth to the titillating tales of Palace intrigues that characterized much of the Dowager Empress Cixi's reign.

I saw the small *well* where she had apparently dumped the favorite concubine of the emperor and left her to die, when the upstart girl seemed to have effectively ingratiated herself to the emperor, to the extent that she had become a threat to the Dowager Empress's influence.

The Empress Dowager Cixi

had started her career in the Palace as a low ranking concubine to the Ching Xian Feng emperor, to whom she bore a son. Upon the emperor's death in 1862, Cixi had become empress mother and co‑ regent for the new young emperor. She soon became adept in the use of the royal prerogative of appointment and dismissal, to an extent which allowed her to consolidate her power and influence at court.

When we arrived at her living quarters, it was explained to me that she had invited the most learned of feng shui masters to protect and preserve her imperial authority.

Though small, her apartments had supposedly been lavishly decorated with symbols of longevity and power. Many of these precious objects had long ago been taken away, but I could see that the entrance to her room opened into a beautiful small courtyard which must have symbolized her personal *bright hall.*

More significantly, the empress Cixi had been born an East group person, (1835) and her most auspicious directions had been North/South/East and Southeast. As a result the all important north/south axis of the entire Palace complex had been extremely auspicious for her. All the important gates, entrances and halls faced north or south. Cixi benefited tremendously from this orientation because the chi that flowed into the palaces all brought beneficial, protective and auspicious good fortune to her.

In the closing decades of the Ching dynasty, Cixi became all powerful, but she never ruled directly Her power was always wielded from *behind the curtain,* and she did not relinquish control of the country, right until her death in 1908.

Based on her date of birth, and according to the Pa Ku Lo Shu Compass formula, the Palace complex had endowed her with monumental earth luck. Her feng shui was enormously auspicious, and there was no way she would have been defeated by any of her enemies. Perhaps that is why she stayed all powerful throughout her life, and up to her death.

The living quarters of the emperors

I also saw the official living quarters of the emperors and empresses in the Inner Court where they supposedly resided in the Palaces of Earthly Tranquillity and Heavenly Purity. The imperial concubines also lived in the Inner Court, in six palaces on the east and six on the west side.

The imperial bridal chamber was located in the Palace of Earthly Tranquillity and here I saw the lavish use of the double happiness symbol, the Chinese word *xi* repeated.

 This word (shown here on the left) is always associated with conjugal bliss, and in the emperor's bedroom, this auspicious symbol was incorporated into pierced lattice screens, and painted red on lanterns that were hung from lavishly decorated ceilings. I was later to find out that this *double happiness* symbol is regarded as extremely effective when placed (in any form) in the marriage corner of bedrooms. It is however most effective when coloured red !

The imperial marriage bed was constructed in an alcove, and was shielded by multi coloured embroidered see through silk curtains depicting *one hundred children* playing. This is a traditional theme sewn onto silks or drawn on paintings to be made as gifts to newly weds, implicitly symbolizing many descendants for the recipients.

Both of the principal Palaces of the Inner Court, because they were the living quarters of the emperors and empresses, were placed on the *central north/south axis*. And together with the three Great Audience Halls of the Outer Court (equivalent to throne rooms) these buildings form the heart of the Forbidden City.

Feng Shui shapes and dimensions.

The City itself demonstrated important basic rules of feng shui. All halls, rooms and palaces, and in fact the entire City complex were regular in shape. Palaces and Halls were either rectangular or square. As were pavilions and courtyards.

Many of the pavilions and ceiling designs also bore the auspicious eight sided shape of the Pa Kua.

Bricks used in the construction of the Palace complex were almost all square, and <u>roof shapes</u> followed strict feng shui proportions and dimensions.

Altogether there were nine different types of roof shapes used in the Forbidden City. These are generally regarded as auspicious designs, and can be seen to have been used also in temples and other important buildings throughout the rest of the country.

In the old days, the use of specific shapes, designs or colours used by the imperial family were often forbidden to the common people except with the consent of the emperor. Not everyone could so easily use or practice feng shui !

Roof shapes of Palaces and Buildings in the Forbidden City

1. Single eaved pitched roof   2. Double eaved hipped roof
3. Double eaved hipped roof with gablets   4. Half hipped flat topped roof
5. Pitched roof   6. Pitched roof with overhanging eaves   7. Rolled pitched roof
8.   Conical roof 9. Hipped pavilion roof

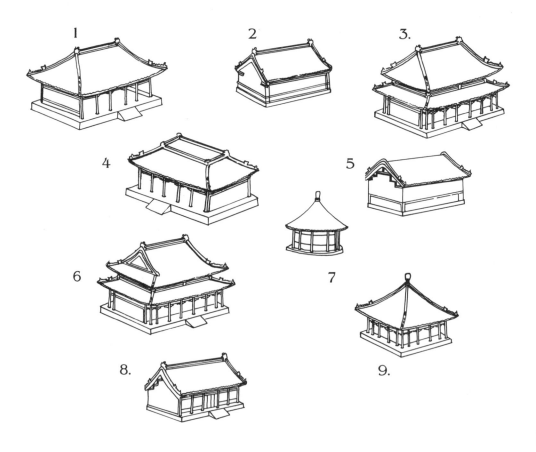

Feng Shui Layout and Orientation of the Forbidden City

This sketch of the Forbidden City shows the significant feng shui features which had been incorporated into the layout and construction of the palaces of the Forbidden City. The entrance was the <u>Meridien Gate</u> which <u>faced South</u> (supposedly an auspicious direction). The north/south central axis of the major buildings reflect the imperial nature of the residence. At the back, in the North is <u>Prospect Hill</u>, an artificially created hillock that symbolizes the protective Turtle hills. The young princes of the realm lived in the palaces in the East (to symbolize youth and growth). In the centre of the complex, which symbolized earth, and from which all things spring, are the three halls and the two palaces, the heart of the city where the emperor lived and worked. The Palaces of Tranquil Old Age and of Longevity are located in the North West which symbolized the powerful trigram *chien*. Here elders lived. Walls of the City, and especially along the South are painted red to reflect the symbolism of South's fire element, while roof tiles are in the imperial yellow, except in the east, where roof tiles are green to symbolize wood, which is the element of the East.

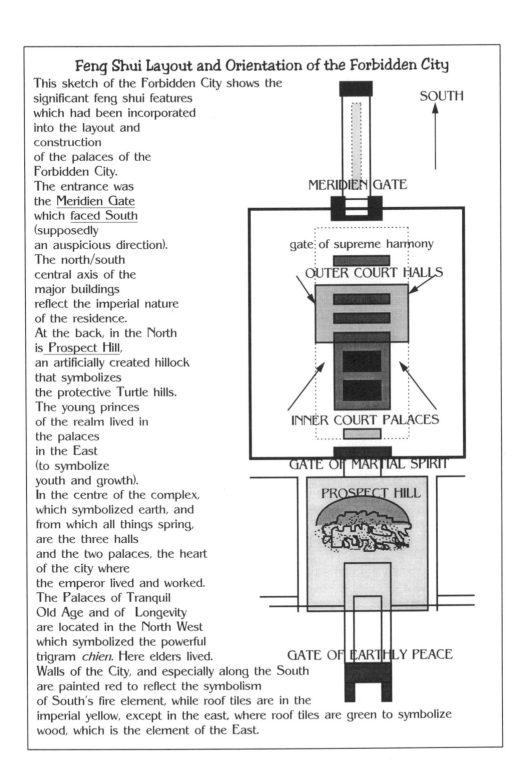

SOUTH

MERIDIEN GATE

gate of supreme harmony

OUTER COURT HALLS

INNER COURT PALACES

GATE OF MARTIAL SPIRIT

PROSPECT HILL

GATE OF EARTHLY PEACE

Flow of water in the Forbidden City

One aspect of my tour of the Forbidden City which was of considerable interest was the arrangement of the flow of water within the complex. I had been constantly reminded that both *wind* and *water* or feng shui had been taken into account each time succeeding generations of architects had drawn up new or renovation plans for the imperial City.

I was told that the overall placement of the Palaces and the flow of water in the complex had been drawn to conform to the *Canon of Dwellings,* one of the older texts on feng shui which contained a specific set of rules concerning orientation according to the terrain and conditions of the site.

According to this old text, building orientation should be determined *according to the directions of the sun and the wind.* So that in the winter months buildings are exposed to the sun and sheltered from the wind, while in the summer it is away from the direction of the wind.

A good site, my guide told me, *is one that is backed by hills and faces water* ! Thus the city of Beijing, for instance, is sheltered by the *Yan Shan* mountains to the North, with the *Bo Hai* sea in the east. The ground rises to the north and falls away south. The city thus has the advantage of both good exposure and drainage.

The Forbidden City too demonstrates this important feature. In terms of ground level, it is higher in the North than the South by over a meter ! And in order to achieve the rule of *mountains behind, water in front,* earth excavated for the river (or artificial water) was piled up at the back of the City in the North to form Longevity Hill, and further along also Prospect Hill.

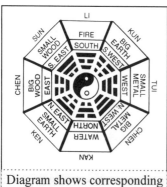

Diagram shows corresponding directions & trigrams

Meanwhile a river, named Golden river to reflect its origination in the Northwest (which is symbolized by the element metal or gold) was also created to have water in front of the palace complex ! The *origination, exit* and *direction of flow* of this river was supposedly designed to conform to ancient environmental design or feng shui.
In the case of the Forbidden City, the feng shui masters in the court of the Ming emperors had determined that water should come from the *chien* direction.

The HARVARD B SCHOOL YEARS

Picture above ... with my roommate, Parmelee Eastman at the Harvard Business School, winter of 1975. We shared a tiny apartment in Hamilton Hall.
Picture below ... My room at Hamilton Hall where I fell desperately ill with pneumonia and pleurisy .... and only recovered after I changed my sleeping directions.

The ARRIVAL OF JENNIFER

It was only after we had moved out of our Kenny Hills home and into our own house in Pantai Hills that we succeeded in having a baby ! Jennifer arrived in the summer of 1977 after we had both given up hope of ever having a child ... this wonderful new development in my life was to make me take a second, more serious look at feng shui ... for the Pantai Hills house had been specially designed to activate our family corner, and more specifically my husband's *nien yen* corner.

As can be seen from this family picture taken soon after Jennifer was born, we truly enjoyed our life then ... whether or not it was due to good feng shui, how are we to know ... but it was nearly ten years after we married before she finally came ... and I was not then under medical treatment of any kind ... in fact we were not even trying ... Picture below shows me and my baby in the garden of our Pantai Hills home, where we still live except it has since been renovated and expanded. The pond behind us is now inside the house.

The HONG LEONG YEARS

This was my office when I started working for Hong Leong. It was small but I was later to discover how auspicious it was for me. The shelves on my right did not hurt me, and my directions were near perfect ... two years later I moved to another larger office which had to be completely redone to improve the feng shui. Here I am negotiating a US$64 million dollar loan with the Wardley guys from Singapore ... Nick and Andrew Todd. On my right, James Davies from the London solicitors firm, Freshfields. Notice how bankers negotiate with champagne.!

The HONG LEONG YEARS

I loved my corporate career with the Hong Leong Group and have much to be grateful for in meeting up with Quek Leng Chan, the brilliant Chairman and moving force behind this fast moving conglomerate. He was both mentor and boss and I enjoyed a wonderful relationship with him. Picture above, I am with his brother Kwek Leng Hai and him at a cocktail in Hong Kong; and below, toasting with then President of the MCA Dato Lee San Choon, and Minister Mak Hon Kam at one of our Group annual dinners in Kuala Lumpur. Those were fun days!

The HONG LEONG YEARS

Scenes from my corporate working days. Above, photographed with colleagues and fellow directors of the Group's management company in the Hong Leong penthouse in Jalan Bandar in downtown Kuala Lumpur, and below one of many group pictures taken in the course of my work. Here, we are in the Group's Boardroom in Hong Kong, October 1984, after signing the joint venture agreement with the Fujian Province Enterprise Corporation of China to build a hotel in Fuzhou. Negotiating with the mainland Chinese was tough work !

TAKING OVER AT DAO HENG BANK IN HONG KONG

We celebrated the official takeover of Dao Heng Bank with a dragon dance, believed to be auspicious, and we had the then Commissioner of Banking, Colin Martin unveil our new logo. Note the Hong Leong dragon, now redrawn (without the confining circle) and holding on to a coin to signify great prosperity. On my right is Mr Quek Leng Chan, Chairman of the Bank, and also Executive Chairman of the giant Hong Leong Group of Malaysia.

The DAO HENG BANK YEARS

Picture above ... the Chairman and I, giving *lai see* or red packets to the staff to mark the happiness of the occasion.
Picture below ... my office in 1985. Note the white building on my left which was supposed to symbolize the *white tiger* ...except that it was on the wrong side!

The DAO HENG BANK YEARS

Picture above ... Opening of the bank's new branch in Tsuen Wan was celebrated with a dragon dance to attract auspicious luck and harmony.
Picture below ... leading a contingent of over 400 Bank staff at the Community Chest charity big walk, an annual event. With me were Vivian Lee and David Kiang, both General managers at the bank, and also adviser Frank Tung.

VISITS TO CHINA IN THE EIGHTIES
In March 1985 I visited the Great Wall of China with my Dao Heng Bank colleagues, Kwek Leng San, who was general manager in charge of Treasury, and Frank Tung, son of the bank's original Founder who was then adviser to the Board. We were in Beijing at the invitation of the Bank of China.

Picture on top shows me with Kwek on my right and Frank Tung on my left. The visit to the Great Wall was a horrendously moving experience. It snaked for thousands of miles, and we could not help but think of the millions of men who died building the Wall. I felt so much sorrow there, and I do not want to ever again visit the place. The picture below was taken at the Forbidden Palace.

VISITS TO CHINA IN THE EIGHTIES

In May 1985 I visited Beijing again, this time to attend the Euromoney Conference on the "Future of China". This time I went with Kwek Leng Hai who had succeeded me as Managing Director at Dao Heng Bank while I had moved on to become Managing Director and partner at Hong Leong Securities. Picture shows me at the entrance to the Great Hall of the People with Tian An Men Square in the background.. Picture below, taken with T.Y. Wang, who by then had become President of the Bank of China and Ahmet Arsan, Managing Director of International Bank of Asia ... we were attending a dinner in the Summer palace outside Beijing hosted by the Arab Banking Corporation.

PARTNERSHIP WITH CYNTHIA

My great friend and partner, Cynthia Picazo, like me, a former Banker who also wanted to get out of the financial world and do something different. Cynthia had been Chief Executive of the Phillipines based PCI's finance company in Hong Kong. An MBA graduate from Wharton School of Finance, we had known each other for years. She had been my shopping mate for a long time before we started our first boutique together ... Je - Anne ! (picture below shows opening of the boutique which turned out to be one of those social occasions ... where we invited all the rich ladies of Hong Kong. With me are Sheila Poon, Dickson Poon's mother, Mrs David Li, and Yvonne Boey.

The picture on the right shows Cynthia seated at her new office, as Managing Director of Dragon Seed, the acquisition we successfully engineered together when we decided that running a small boutique was not exactly what we had in mind when we decided to go into business together.
We had to get down to work almost immediately after the acquisition in January of 1987, but the first thing we did was to have the feng shui of the place checked out to make certain we got our feng shui right.

THE DRAGON SEED YEARS

We created Hong Kong's most beautiful Home and Design Centre and for its grand opening on the 4th July 1987, America's Independence day we flew TV soap opera star Morgan Fairchild to Hong Kong to lend glamour to the occasion. But I also had a magnificent 100 feet dragon dance !! Pictures show the occasion, graced by representatives of our financiers, Michael Kwee from Prudential Asia and Manny Pangilinan from the First Pacific Group.

THE DRAGON SEED YEARS

In the Autumn of 1987, we opened HEIRESS, our up market boutique that sold the most expensive designer wear from Paris and Milan, targeted at the rich *tai tai* market of Hong Kong. The store was visually stunning and the products were luxurious and beautiful beyond words ... but we had compromised on location in the sense that the building we had selected had a history of failures due to poor feng shui. We had been desperate to look for a suitable place big enough in the Central district of Hong Kong island ... Business was not good, and even after feng shui changes were made, the store barely broke even. I learnt never to compromise on feng shui again after that experience. On the right, me and Cynthia toasting the opening of HEIRESS, and below the fashion floor.

SHOPPING TILL WE DROPPED !

The whole of 1987 and 1988, Cynthia and I travelled and shopped till we literally dropped ! Paris, Milan, Florence, Venice, Bologna, Frankfurt, London, New York ... in search of the best and the most exquisite products for our chain of department stores and boutiques ... as self appointed top buyers for Dragon Seed department store we shopped like empresses, and travelled through the fashion capitals of the world. By the end of 1988, the sheer hard work and leg work had worn us down to the extent that we were asking if all this hard work was really all worth while ... pictures below taken in Paris with my suppliers ... top, with Emmanuelle Khanh at her Salon in Hugo Street, and below with Claude Havrey marketing director Isabella Lehman and group picture with Frederic Malraux and Jean Marlaix, owners of the house of La Bagagerie ....

MEETING THE MOST CREATIVE PEOPLE IN THE WORLD !

In Italy we found the most exquisite home products, the best leather fashion shoes, and the most wonderful gold and fake jewellery. Shown here are pictures taken with Renato and Patrizia Cenedella, one of the best shoe suppliers from Bologna; and with the Marioni family who made stunning art objects in ceramics and Marielli Innocent, designer of exquisite jewellery, both from Firenze In Rome we also met the lovely Gina Lollobrigida who entertained us with stories of her great admiration for Fidel Castro and her intense dislike of Imelda Marcos !

BACK TO MALAYSIA TO A NEW CAREER !

I retired from the corporate world, sold out of Dragon Seed and came home to Malaysia as soon as I realised Jennifer had reached the age when having a full time mother was vital. In 1993 I came out with my first book on feng shui, which became a huge local bestseller. Much encouraged I started to write in earnest and to date have penned a total of nine bestsellers, five of them on the wonderful science of feng shui. With Yap Cheng Hai, (with me in pictures below) I wrote books on specific feng shui formulas, vital gems of my Chinese traditional heritage which we felt should not be lost. Pictures below show the official launching of my first book on Feng Shui by MCA President and Minister of Transport, Datuk Seri Dr. Ling Liong Sik, and the launching of my fifth book .... on Water Feng Shui by Minister of Housing, Datuk Dr. Ting Chew Pei.

This is *Northwest* based on the Later Heaven Arrangement of the Pa Kua. The water was supposed to flow out of the complex in the *sun* direction which is *Southeast*.

Thus the inner river in the Forbidden City leads in from the Northwest, winds southwards through the western flank of the Hall of Military Eminence and then turns East to the front of the gate of Supreme Harmony and travels from west to east. It leaves the City in the Southeast corner of the Forbidden City, to correspond to the Trigram *sun* in the Pa Kua.

I asked my guide if this flow of water symbolized the famous *water dragon* referred to in the *Water Dragon Classic* but he was not able to tell me. However, I later discovered that the reason the water originated from the Northwest was because this part of the Palace complex corresponded to the Trigram *chien*, which means *heaven*.

The emperor is regarded as the *son of heaven* and water coming from heaven was thus deemed fitting and right for the abode of the emperor !

Yong Le the Ming Emperor responsible for rebuilding the northern capital. He was the emperor who proclaimed that construction work was to be started on the new imperial palace in Beijing by the fifth month of the year 1407. Officials were dispatched to the provinces to gather building materials. Craftsmen, soldiers and commoners were conscripted. The Forbidden City complex took thirteen years to build and was completed in 1420. In the following year, three major halls in the Outer Court were destroyed by fire, and the next year one of the palaces in the Inner Court was also burnt down. Yong Le died two years later, and it was only in 1436 that plans were drawn up to rebuild the three audience halls of the Outer Court, followed by the Palace of the Inner Court three years later. All through the reigns of the ten Ming emperors that followed Yong Le, there was to be continuos reconstruction of the various buildings of the City. The Ching Dynasty moved in, in 1644 .....

Another explanation may have been due to the fact that the Forbidden City possessed no natural surface supplies of water of its own, so that water had to be channeled into the City from the *Great Water Pool* in the northwest. It was from this pool that water ran southward and entered the Inner Court where it then became the Golden River as it passed from west to east across the courtyard inside the Meridian Gate. Reaching the Southeast it reemerged from the city to converge with the *Changpu, Imperial and Tong hui rivers.*

Whatever the reason, the emperor Yong Le's reign was followed by ten emperors and the Ming dynasty lasted for another 238 years ! This surely has to be considered as good enough feng shui ?

Yin and Yang balance in the Forbidden City

The architectural design of the Forbidden City directly reflects the principles of *yin* and *yang,* which is regarded as the way of heaven and earth. The yin/yang principle suggests that everything can be divided into two mutually opposing and independent components, each signifying either *yin* or *yang.* This *unity of opposites* theory found expression in the layout of the City as well as in the number of buildings, doors and gates of the Inner and Outer Courts. The cardinal rule followed was the attainment of *yin/yang* balance so that auspicious and harmonious *chi* would at all times prevail.

Later I was to discover that the principles of *yin* and *yang* formed one of the pillars of good feng shui practice, and that the difficulty lay in getting the balance just right. It is possible, and indeed quite easy to learn the basic manifestations of these two opposing forces ‑ this is simply a matter of research.

Thus the sun is y*ang* while the moon is *yin;* just like light and life and daytime hours are *yang,* while darkness and death are *yin,* and so it goes ... what is difficult in the achievement of feng shui harmony is to introduce just the right amount of *yang (or yin)* into the living space based on the nature of room usage and overall environmental influences.

It was also pointed out to me that there is a difference between *Yin feng shui* and *Yang feng shui.* Yin feng shui had to do with the eternal resting places of ancestors, the dwellings of the dead. In the old days, this vital aspect of a family's feng shui was closely monitored by family elders, as it was believed that good *yin feng shui* benefited descendants. The apparently excellent configuration of hills that surround the Ming Tombs reflect imperial practice of *Yin feng shui.*

That the dynasty collapsed in the sixteen forties, I was told indicated the effect of other intangible energies that manifested the time dimension of feng shui ... it was also suggested that the last Ming emperor had become careless, thereby ignoring the practice of annually checking up on the feng shui of his ancestors' tombs !

I was actually also told about a family that lived in Guanzhou whose ancestral burial grounds was so well tended and had such excellent *yin feng shui* that the family has prospered for at least fourteen generations, and continues to prosper till today, its descendants living through the turmoil of China's history, yet somehow surviving and continually thriving ... I had attempted several times to locate and make contact with this family, whose present day patriarch, I was told was a very high ranking official, but never succeeded in doing so.

Yang feng shui concerned the houses of the living, and practicing this branch of feng shui is considerably easier and more practical in the modern context. I have to confess that I focused only on learning *yang feng shui,* and my books deal only with this aspect of the subject.

The five elements
It was while touring the Forbidden City that I came to understand the theory of *wu xing* or five elements. My guide kept pointing to this palace and that palace and saying, here is where the princes lived and see, it is of the wood element so you can see why the roof tiles here are green; or see, the walls here are painted red, that is because it symbolizes the element fire.

I had to ask him to explain *wu xing* to me, and of course when he did I realized I had come across it many times, only that I had never truly understood the dynamics of the element relationships, or of its premier place in feng shui rationale. Mr Zheng informed me that Chinese architecture closely followed this theory of the five elements.

It is a very ancient concept, Mr Zheng explained, *and it is mentioned in almost all the old history books.* Apparently books as old as 2500 years ago that describe Chou Dynasty history contain detailed explanations of the nature of the Five elements, which listed in order thus ‒ water, fire, wood, metal/gold and earth ‒ represent the five different kinds of matter that people frequently come in contact with. But it is of course the essence of the elements rather than the elements themselves, which in combination cause all things, good or bad, to occur.

Thus in the wrong combination, they are mutually destructive and can cause great distress to human life, while the correct combination would create enormous happiness !

So how does one go about understanding the elements and using this knowledge in feng shui since so many things can be interpreted to represent these elements ! Surely it must be terrifically difficult to get the combinations correct. Indeed it is, and usually the best feng shui Masters are those whose knowledge of elements is deep and substantial.

The most significant categories for feng shui purposes, are the compass direction equivalents of the elements. Thus East is wood, south is fire, west is metal, north is water and the center is earth ! And then there are the colour representations of the elements. Green is wood, red is fire, white is metal, black/blue is water and yellow is earth !
Everything can be classified into these five categories ... emotions, the weather, musical notes, even stages of life. But how to interpret them for feng shui analysis ?

Well, Mr Zheng pointed out examples of the use of <u>colours</u> and <u>allocation of rooms</u> in the Forbidden Palace which he explained reflected the five element theory at work.
Perhaps one could learn by seeing examples of its application !

Thus, of the five colours, *green* being the color of sprouting leaves, it symbolizes the advent of Spring and corresponds to the East. Following this pattern, major buildings in the Eastern part of the Forbidden City such as the Hall of Literary Glory, where the young princes studied were originally covered with green glazed tiles. This was later replaced with yellow tiles when the Hall was used for other purposes. Green tiles were also used in the official residences of the princes built during the Chien Lung period. Green roof tiles were used because in the stages of life according to the five elements, youth is signified by wood and corresponded to the East direction !

Similarly because the empress dowager and the concubines of the emperor would usually be older, their stages of life correspond to *metal* and the *west.* Thus empresses usually lived in the rooms of the west wing of the complex. When I examined the names of the palaces closely, indeed I saw that all the *old sounding* Palaces ... like the Palace of Peace and Old Age; of Longevity and Good Health, and of Compassion and Tranquillity - these were all meant for older members of the Imperial family and were thus located in the west.

Further examples of the input of element theory can also be gleaned in the colours of tiles used. Thus at the Altar of Earth and Grain, I noticed that the terraces and walls surrounding the altar were covered with different coloured tiles; green in the east, red in the south, white in the west and black in the north, with yellow in the center !

I have gone into some detail about my visits to the Forbidden City simply because I feel it is so significant that the emperors of imperial China as well as their ministers at Court, placed so much consequence on observing feng shui rules and guidelines. It was this revelation that was to make me look at feng shui seriously, and I want to share this with readers.

Later I was to discover that there is a great deal of hypothesis behind the practice of feng shui. Much of modern feng shui contain variations and different interpretations of the old texts, and I was to learn also that not all the old texts were necessarily authentic .... As readers will see when they get to the story of the emperor who founded the Ming dynasty itself .... Chu Yuan Chang, the emperor who believed his elevation to the dragon throne had been due to good feng shui, and who as a result, wished to forever deprive everyone else in the kingdom from having access to the science ...

CHAPTER NINE
TALES FROM THE MIDDLE KINGDOM
How authentic are the ancient texts ?

I am never surprised when readers express frustration at conflicting feng shui advice. There are indeed different schools of feng shui practice and their sometimes contrary approaches can give rise to confusion. While it helps to approach the subject in a systematic and scientific way, this is not always easy to do. It also does not help that their are different compass school formulas of feng shui, and when computations throw up different recommendations it can be frustrating.

I have always advised practitioners that feng shui is as old as most things Chinese. Some say it began eons ago when the ancient classic, the I Ching was first written ... this would make feng shui as old as four thousand years ... I prefer to think of feng shui as having been started during the Tang Dynasty simply because some of the earliest recorded texts which refer to feng shui, or something like feng shui appeared during the Tang dynasty which ruled China between the seventh and tenth century.

Tang dynasty feng shui was of the form (or landscape) school. This makes references to the lay of the land, the terrain, the shape of mountains, the flow of rivers and the direction of wind flows ...

Feng shui texts however, seldom described environmental forms directly. References to hills and mountains were always represented as either dragons or tigers, turtles or phoenixes ... and shapes of hills, and flows of rivers, were described as being either *fire, water, metal, wood or earth* - the five elements. Often also, various types of good feng shui were described with reference to popular legends - phrases like ... *being cradled in the palm of the moon goddess* or *sitting on the eternal pearl of the dragon* ... and while these meant good feng shui, they often made little sense to those ignorant of the stories behind the legends.

Looking at the revival of feng shui in our age, and surveying the amount of literature now available, I am all too aware of the *spread* of different feng shui systems ... So I went in search of explanations, and together, Yap Cheng Hai and myself compared the differences in the contrary systems of computations. In the process we discovered many of these differences to be superficial, and when we dug a little deeper, there would always be explanations for the so called differences.

We discovered that much of the differences had to do with interpretations of the five element relationships, and in the significance placed on the use of different good fortune symbols ... in short, there was little which could not be rationalized. We also found that dialect differences accounted for the use of different symbols.

Much of feng shui's explanations made sense when we went back to its source books, principally the I Ching ...

What was interesting however, when we went in search of explanations for the different theories of feng shui, was a story we dug up about the authenticity of feng shui texts itself, a story which forced us to question the authenticity of texts that directly contradict the application methods related to the Pa Kua's trigrams. ... it is a story that takes us back to the fourteenth century ...

The story of the first Ming emperor...

In the year 1368, a man from the peasant classes founded the Ming Dynasty which ruled China for 276 years ... Chu Yang Chang was a *garrulous, ugly man who had protruding eyes, a double chin and black spots all over his face.* He was born on a farm and came from the poorest and lowest of backgrounds of all the founding emperors of China. But from young, he had apparently demonstrated a spirit so courageous, he had become something of a local hero in his village.

Books describe how he had led bands of village boys stealing chickens and cows and committing other acts of youthful outrage, and when caught, while his companions ran away in fear of reprisals, he would stoically own up and endure the beatings on behalf of his friends. Later he spent some years as a beggar, and later masqueraded as a monk.

Chu lived by his wits, and survived by the strength of his spirit and the excellence of his fighting skills.

And then, so the story goes, his father passed away. Chu prided himself on being a filial son, and determined to give his father a proper burial, he single handedly dragged his father's coffin up the winding roads outside the village, and into the mountains. His intention was to reach a spot half way up the mountain, a place where the poorer farmers of the village buried their dead ... except that halfway through the journey, the skies darkened, the ground shook and the rains came.

A huge and terrific storm descended upon the entire mountain.

Unable to continue, and fearing for his life, Chu dropped the coffin and fled back to the village. The storm persisted for three days and three nights, and by the time it cleared, Chu realized that an entire face of the mountain had crumbled, totally burying his father's coffin.

The dragons had intervened and the mountain landslide had provided his father a permanent resting place.

And it was following this incident, so popular folklore says, that Chu became a warlord, leading an increasingly expanding army that ultimately defeated the imperial forces of the Mongol rulers of the Yuan dynasty ... thus it was that in 1368, Chu Yuan Chang installed himself as the first ruler of the Ming Dynasty.

He named his reign Hong Wu which in Chinese is roughly translated to mean *big and strong and powerful* ... but all the trappings of imperial splendor could not assuage Chu's own feelings of insecurity. He saw plotters and schemers where there were none, and during his reign, he ordered fierce purges of his closest generals. In all there were three major massacres which saw him cut down even his closest confidantes ...

It must have been this same sense of insecurity which later led him to pass the imperial edict forbidding anyone from practicing feng shui. Having been told that it was the excellent feng shui of his father's burial place which had catapulted him onto the throne of China, he reasoned that if feng shui was indeed so powerful, then no one save him should have access to the knowledge.

Thus he ordered his scholars to flood the kingdom with books that contained misleading theories and wrong guidelines on feng shui, so that no one would be able to use feng shui to topple him !
It is surmised that one of his descendants, the third Ming emperor whose reign year was known as Yong Le indeed followed the guidelines of one of these misleading books to build the palaces of the present Forbidden City ... and that was how two years after the first palaces were built, two of them caught fire and were razed to the ground.

And it was only in succeeding periods that the genuine authentic books were recovered, and proper geomantic guidelines followed.
The architectural history of the Palaces of the Forbidden City are thus strewn with incidents that tell of whole Palace wings being burnt to the ground.

There continued to be much rebuilding throughout the reign of the Mings, and later the Chings; but in the labyrinth of courtyards, palaces and rooms of the Forbidden City still standing today, evidence of the application of feng shui symbolism and feng shui orientations abound.

But the question remains: how many of those misleading texts made their way through the kingdom ... and how are we to know which contains the genuine and which the fake feng shui principles ? Which leads me also to ask the question *How authentic are the ancient texts on feng shui* ?

The rise of Dr. Sun Yat Sen

The feng shui stories that come out of China often refer to *yin* feng shui, which many believe is much more potent that *yang* feng shui. This has its explanation in part to the importance placed on ancestor worship, and in part to the belief that *yin* feng shui has to do with heavenly forces; as opposed to the less powerful earth forces which is harnessed by *yang* feng shui.

Yin feng shui is the feng shui of ancestral grave sites. Feng shui masters of the old school place great importance on the orientation and location of the ancestral burial site. They maintain that if one's ancestors enjoy auspicious feng shui in their final resting places, then only can the descendants prosper and rise to prominence.

Indeed it is believed that if the ancestral burial grounds are correctly orientated according to the auspicious *green dragon, white tiger configuration,* then the sons of the family will enjoy great wealth and attain high positions of influence and power in their careers.

There is no wider quoted story to back this than that of the rise to prominence and power of the founder of the Kuomintang or Nationalist party <u>Dr. Sun Yat Sen.</u> Dr. Sun has long been acknowledged as the father of the Chinese republic. He was born to humble peasants in a village near Canton in 1866. Like many families in the region, his family had allowed the eldest son, his elder brother, to migrate abroad, and Dr. Sun's brother emigrated to Honolulu. Thus it was that Dr. Sun spent some years studying in Hawaii. Later, he returned to Hong Kong where he completed his medical studies. His overseas exposure gave rise to a revolutionary zeal that would eventually lead to the 1911 revolution that toppled the Manchu reign of China, thereby forever changing the history of modern China.
What gave Dr. Sun the edge ?

What was it which made him succeed where earlier reformists like Kang Yu Wei, and even the sacked emperor Kuang Su (sacked by his aunt, the empress dowager Cixi, when he tried to introduce changes) whose Society for the Protection of the Emperor in San Francisco seemed at first to hold out promise of change for China, could not.

How was it that at the turn of the century, it was Sun Yat Sen who became the most popular personality around which many anti royalists clamored ?

How was it that a Christian, a western educated doctor, and not someone more likely, who would become the rallying point around which resonated the call for the overthrow of the dynasty.

Not only did he attract support from within China, Sun Yat Sen's revolution was also supported by overseas Chinese, many of whom responded with ardor, allegiance, and money. Thus did the Nationalists eventually succeed in toppling the Manchus.

The answer, once again according to popular folklore was feng shui ... yin feng shui, because it was due to the excellent orientation of his mother's grave. This was lyrically described to me in the early Eighties as I sat sipping tea in a hotel in Canton, with associates of mine.

One of the Chinese guests who sat with us was someone from the mayor's office, whose name I do not now recall. I had mentioned that Dr. Sun was from Canton. *Did anyone ever hear about his mother's grave,* I asked, *being reputed to enjoy such excellent feng shui, it had brought great good fortune to the second son ?*

And immediately the story was taken up. Frank Tung who was a fellow director of mine on the Board of Dao Heng Bank nodded eloquently, indicating that he too had heard the story. It was then that the gentleman from Canton intervened.

Yes he said, *Dr. Sun's mother's grave was located high on one of the mountains overlooking the sea. It was nestled,* he said, *in exactly the spot where the green dragon embraced the precious pearl,* a most auspicious orientation, and Chinese from far and wide often nod knowingly whenever they speak of Dr. Sun, referring to him as having been spawned of the dragon ... thus was he granted the mandate to topple the upstart foreign rulers ⁻ the Manchus !

There are other stories that tell of ancestral feng shui in the same vein, especially regarding China's modern day rulers. This same gentleman from Canton told us a story he had heard about how Generalissimo Chiang Kai Shek, the ruthless leader of the Kuomintang, went to great lengths to learn about Mao Tze Tung's feng shui.

How, at the height of his struggle with the communists for the hearts and minds of the Chinese people, he would kidnap anyone known to have been close to Mao Tze Tung, and how he had them tortured to pry from them, the location of the ancestral grave of Mao's grandfather.

Chiang Kai Shek was apparently an ardent believer of feng shui, and having learnt that Mao's ancestral burial ground was located *sitting on the palm of the moon goddess ...* he believed that to defeat Mao he would have to destroy Mao's ancestral feng shui. He never found it of course, and Mao himself would indeed emerge victorious and eventually become the new emperor of China.

In later years, Mao Tze Tung's personal living space and feng shui was to become the subject of much speculation. It was whispered that Mao was superstitious, and in the early days of his victory, he avoided staying in Zhongnanhai until, so the story goes, the feng shui of the place had been improved.

A superstitious Mao

It is reputed that Mao was extremely superstitious. It was said when he was a teenager, someone had predicted he would one day become a great leader ... then years later, during the days of the Long March, he had visited the Chingling monastery on the banks of the Yellow river, forty miles east of Yanan. There a Taoist monk had apparently prostrated himself at Mao's feet and *declared:*

You are a real dragon son of heaven.

Intrigued Mao had urged the monk to be more explicit in his prophecy, whereupon the monk told him that he would indeed go on to Beijing, and that he would found a new dynasty on October 1st. It was a prophecy that was to come uncannily true for on that exact date in 1949, Mao stood proudly with his comrades of the Long March, above the Gate of Heavenly Peace in Tiananmen Square, and proclaimed the founding of the People's Republic, raised the new flag of China and sang the new anthem. Thus began a new era and anew dynasty for China.

Contrary to widely held beliefs, Mao looked more to China's past than to the Communism of Lenin and Karl Marx for his ideas of Government. He seemed to prefer learning from China's classics, and the rise and fall of the past emperors fascinated him. His personal library contained volumes on Chinese dynastic rule, and in particular he read especially the *Twenty Four Annals of the Dynasties*, which comprised much of the history of the Chinese empire.

So it is not surprising that Mao believed also in feng shui. To start with, Mao held the conviction that the Forbidden City, with its North South axis, would be unsuitable and inauspicious for him. Mao had been born in the year of the *water snake*, and his KUA number was 7 making him very much a <u>West group</u> person. The directions and orientations of the Forbidden City were deadly for him from a feng shui viewpoint .... Forewarned, he never set foot there. Later, he had apparently told his courtiers *I am an earth dragon, not a sky dragon.*

In Chinese mythology only the *sky dragon* lived in the imperial city. And indeed, in those early days of the People's Republic the communists seriously considered razing the imperial palaces to the ground. Ideologues hated the Forbidden City. For them it symbolized imperial decadence. Luckily for posterity, the Forbidden City was left alone !

Mao's quarters in Zhongnanhai
When he first entered Beijing, Mao spent the spring and summer in the Fragrant Hills before eventually moving into permanent quarters in Zhongnanhai, a complex of palaces which had been left vacant for many years. Mao chose an exquisite Ching Palace built during the 17th century and located in the Garden of Abundance. The Northeast wing of this palace, complete with russet red walls and auspicious yellow roof tiles that had swallow wings was meticulously renovated for Mao. The place had once housed the imperial library and Mao considered this previous usage to symbolize excellent feng shui. Mao prided himself as being something of an intellectual and indeed spent most of his time sprawled in bed and surrounded by books that described previous dynastic rules.

In front of this peaceful abode, wide windows opened onto a pillared terrace and a flat stone courtyard which represented the auspicious bright hall. Beside the courtyard windows, he placed his wooden bed, a square structure that was so large, many described it as a true *emperor bed.* Mao lounged on a mountain of pillows.

He surrounded his bed with lamps and bracket lights to raise the needed *yang* energy. And around the walls of the bedroom, yet more books were placed on shelves. Mao's penchant for old classics was to be a permanent feature of his long reign of China.

Mao's quarters in Zhongnanhai was known as the Study of Chrysanthemum Fragrance. Mao viewed his move into the new quarters with great care, selecting auspicious dates and times ... he regarded it as being his ultimate step into the emperor's chamber. It would signify the official Mandate from heaven !

Mao was obsessed with how each of the *sons of heaven*, the emperors of previous eras came on the throne and how each came to leave it, and he devoured books on the rise and fall of dynasties with great relish. Many books on Mao that have since been published describe him sprawled on his enormous bed, always turning the pages of ancient texts and reading on and on about the transitions from one dynasty to the next ...

Mao's feng shui must have been carefully monitored throughout his stay at Zhongnanhai. For in the end, as we all know, he stayed on the throne until his death, reigning supreme and oblivious to the sufferings of his people even as his most trusted confidants and comrades dropped by the wayside, died or became victims of the Cultural revolution.

That Deng Xio Ping survived and went on to succeed Mao was part of Deng's heaven luck, for like Mao, Deng too would receive the mandate from heaven and eventually ascend the dragon throne of China ... and that is yet another story .

THE TEMPLE OF HEAVEN AT BEIJING. CHINA'S EMPERORS WERE SAID TO RULE BY VIRTUE OF THEIR *MANDATE FEROM HEAVEN*

The funeral of Deng's father

One of my favorite books of recent years is Harrison Salisbury's book THE NEW EMPERORS, a most authoritative and painstakingly researched double biography on Deng Xiao Ping and Mao Tze Tung. Apart from being one of the most alluring and important historical studies about modern China, the book also confirms some interesting stories picked up in Hong Kong, about Deng and Mao's feng shui.

Especially the *yin* feng shui of Deng Xioa Ping ... today's paramount ruler of China. Deng was born in northern Sichuan, in a village whose inhabitants typically believed strongly in superstitious omens. Many of the doors of the village, according to Salisbury, were decorated with red and gold painted figures of armor clad legendary Gods who wielded swords ready to do battle on behalf of the residents. This was indeed a very popular practice amongst old style Chinese, and there are family homes of prominent and successful overseas Chinese whose homes possess this protective door feature.

Deng's father, Deng Wenming was a local strongman who worked closely with one of three local warlords. He had four wives, and they lived in a large home. From the courtyard of the old Deng house, three low, rounded hills are apparently visible. According to feng shui this indicates that the eldest of the sons of the family will rise to great prominence. Deng Xiao Ping was of course the eldest, for although born of the second wife of his father, the first wife had been childless

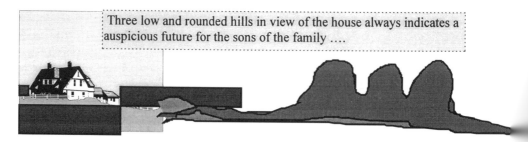

Three low and rounded hills in view of the house always indicates a auspicious future for the sons of the family ....

Others have speculated that the three hills refer directly to the three major upheavals of Deng's political life. Others have interpreted the three hills as merely indicating that the family will be well educated since the three hills represent a pen holder.

Whatever the meaning, it is interesting to note that the presence of three low rounded hills in full view of the house is always a good omen. The local people of Deng's village also point to another omen. They associated Deng's rise to the blooming of a cactus shrub.

This plant, they said, bloomed only once in every hundred years. According to them, in 1979, the year Deng achieved absolute control over China, the plant, located in the courtyard of Deng's family home blossomed for the first time. The villagers of Guangan in Sichuan province saw this as a clear sign that Deng had achieved full power.

Probably the most amazing story of all associated with Deng Xiao Ping's rise to power reminds me of the story about Chu Yang Chuang, the founder of the Ming Dynasty. Apparently in 1940, Deng's father, Deng Wenming was murdered. Like all Chinese of his class and generation, Deng Wenming had selected a site for his grave. But apparently on the day of the funeral, as the procession of mourners carried the coffin to the site, the sky darkened, the wind rose, and exactly as it happened in the case of Chu Yang Chuang's father, the rains came hurtling down, forcing the pall bearers to drop the coffin and run for cover.

Later when the weather had cleared, and the pall bearers returned, they discovered the coffin had got stuck in the mud. They could not move the coffin, and although they were still some *li* (a li is roughly one third of a mile) from the originally selected site, they decided to bury him where the coffin had got stuck. To the superstitious villagers this was read as *the dragon intervening* ...

Later, after Deng had achieved prominence as a high ranking member of the Communist regime, the villagers were to carefully examine the site on which his father had been buried and they saw all sorts of symbolic representations in the hills that surrounded the area.

There were those who described the site as resembling the crimson phoenix, and others pointed also to the range of rounded hills in the distance which signified the auspicious black turtle that would give Deng great longevity and also solid protection throughout his life.

In retrospect, and with the benefit of recent developments, it is tempting to make connections between the various feng shui features spoken of by the villagers and Deng's own life. For of course he enjoys the great good fortune of longevity; just as he did seem also to enjoy a certain amount of divine protection. Where comrades like the all powerful Lui Shao Chi (the President of China) went to an ignominious end during the cultural revolution, Deng did indeed survive even that dangerous period. And today of course he can rightly be regarded as an emperor of China, as perhaps indicated by the burial site of his father.

MODERN FENG SHUI STORIES

ITS ALL IN THE FENG SHUI
Feng shui works whether or not you believe in it
A case of too much water
Descendants luck ... help for childless couples
Enhancing children's luck

ENHANCING YOUR LOVE LIFE WITH FENG SHUI
Improving marriage luck
Can feng shui jazz up your social life ?
Can feng shui help you find a soul mate
Richard and Lyn find love within three months
A feng shui tip for finding your soul mate

ACTIVATING DRAGONS AND TIGERS
Activating the white tiger
Knowing when something is wrong
The Trigram CHIEN attracts mentors
SHENG ... the prosperity hexagram

MODERN FENG SHUI STORIES

THE TUN'S WONDERFUL FENG SHUI
Activating the turtle for longevity and support
'The symbolism of the turtle

FISHY STORIES
...of arrowanas, carps and goldfish
Aquarium of guppies bring job offers galore
Simulating the dragon gate
Displaying the symbol of the dragon/carp

POISON ARROWS CAUSE HAVOC
Sometimes even a tree can create shar chi
Examples of poison arrows in the environment
Summary of feng shui poison arrows
Selecting feng shui cures for blocking poison arrows

Combating shar chi with a cannon
Combating cannon with a large mirror.

CHAPTER 10
IT'S ALL IN THE FENG SHUI
Feng shui works whether or not you believe in it !

Zaiton, a girlfriend of mine (a non believer) complained of massive headaches and annoying problems at the office. She was constantly unwell ! I visited her one day and discovered she was sitting right in front of a massive square pillar. Its sharp edge was pointing directly at her. I suggested she place a plant at the corner of her desk.

She bought one of those creeping plants, and as advised, placed it on her table, and within a week (yes, a week) she not only felt better, she also came into some unexpected money ! For two months everything improved and for the first time she actually felt good about her job. And then things started getting bad again. In desperation she called me. I asked her how the plant was doing.

" *The plant is dying.... what shall I do* ? " she wailed, " *its obvious the plant cannot survive in the enclosed atmosphere of the office* !"

" *Change the plant* " I told her, " *and keep changing the plant every two months !*"

I guess the point of this first story is to remind you from the outset that the practice of feng shui requires a dose of common sense. Solutions are frequently obvious, yet, because of preconceived ideas you do not realize this. In Zaiton's case, she had used the plant to absorb the *shar chi* coming from the sharp edge of the pillar.

Getting *attacked* daily, the plant cannot survive. It will wilt, and eventually die, but by being there, it absorbs the bad *chi* energy, and protects anyone sitting in the direct firing line of the offending pillar. To enjoy continuos protection therefore, Zaiton has to keep replacing the plant; this way the *shar chi* will never hit her !

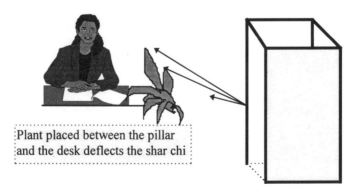

Plant placed between the pillar and the desk deflects the shar chi

A case of too much water ...

In another case, I once visited another friend of mine who had just had the feng shui master in, to improve the feng shui of his office. This gentleman whom I shall call John Tan was the managing director of a publicly listed company.

He had achieved that position when he and his wealthy partner had successfully acquired, and then restructured a listed company. In recent months however, John and his partner had started having serious disagreements. John was unhappy at the speed which his partner seemed to be expanding, and seeing the corporate debts piling up, he had become genuinely worried. Desperate to ensure they did not get pulled into a vortex of debt, John had invited an expensive feng shui master into his office. The feng shui expert declared that what John needed in his office was water, and lots of it !

He suggested that John build a large aquarium. The water, he was told would cool things down at the office, and since John's astrology chart indicated a severe shortage of water in his *basket of elements*, the presence of water would do him a world of good !

John implemented the advice almost immediately and within a week, he had literally surrounded himself with water. In his zeal, John had arranged for an enormous fresh water aquarium to be installed, not just on one side of the room, but right round him ... the fish tank ran all the way from his left hand side, to his back behind him and to his right hand side.

Anyone entering the room would have easily mistaken John's office for a fish aquarium shop, at least that was the first thought that struck me when I went in. I was surprised at what I saw and when I asked John about it, he had shrugged his shoulders. "*feng shui*" he explained, and then proceeded to tell me how the feng shui expert had advised for there to be a strong presence of water. At that time my own expertise in feng shui was not yet a known fact, and I had not started writing my feng shui books ... but of course I knew that while the feng shui advice which John had been given might have been sound, his application was quite amiss.

What John had done was to introduce so much water into his room, it had created a massive imbalance ... oh dear ...

All that water ... far from helping him or bringing him luck, would create massive disharmony in his work space, and quite literally *drown* him ... and indeed that was what happened. Within three months, John was forced to leave the company after he lost out in a Boardroom battle.

The story does not end there ...A few months later, I read that he had accepted the position of managing director of another large company, one that was also listed on the stock exchange, and it seemed that he had recovered from his recent disappointment. John looked set to repeat his success of earlier days ...

Alas for John. He had not learnt his lesson at all.

Once again he installed his giant fish tank ... and once again the water drowned him. John lasted only six months in his new job ! Illustrated here is a sketch plan showing the layout of his room, perfect in every way from a feng shui viewpoint except for the massive fish tank dominating the room !

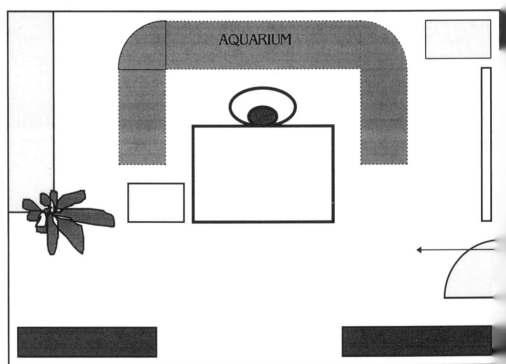

Descendants luck .... help for childless couples ?

The Chinese definition of *luck* comprise many perspectives of the human condition. Thus, while wealth and success represent conspicuous aspirations of mankind, other components of *luck* are equally, if not more important. Probably one of the things nearest and dearest to our hearts then is what I term our *descendants luck*, the welfare and well being of our children ... in short, the next generation. And feng shui, being an ancient Chinese wisdom, directly addresses this by offering ways and means of activating our *descendants luck*.

It fact it was exactly this aspect of feng shui's potency many years ago that first caught my interest. My husband and I had tried desperately to have a child and to start a family soon after our marriage, but Jennifer stubbornly refused to make an appearance, and did not do so until years later, after I had very carefully activated my husband's descendant luck !

This was undertaken on the advice of Yap Cheng Hai ... together we designed the placement of the master bedroom, and oriented my husband's sleeping direction in the new house to ensure that I would get a baby. And it was only then that I succeeded in getting pregnant.

Having been childless for nearly nine years, it seemed like something of a miracle when Jennifer, our daughter was born, just fifteen months after we started living in the new house together.

What we did was activate my husband's *nien yen* luck ie his family luck. This was done by locating the master bedroom in his *nien yen* location ie the South corner of the house, and then arranging the bed to have his head facing his *sheng chi* direction, ie his direction of maximum luck.

The method we used was the *Pa Kua Lo Shu compass formula* which enables everyone to work out their personalized auspicious and inauspicious compass directions and locations, according to the date of birth.

Since then I have discovered how powerful this formula is, and how easy it is to use, for when applied to everyday living it improves one's good fortune in so many different ways. And because it basically involves getting the *sitting, sleeping and working direction* to match with one's favorable directions, it is easy and inexpensive to practice. This formula works equally well for everybody.

My problem was that the formula was so easy, and it seemed so uncomplicated to apply that in the early years there were many moments when I simply forgot (to use it) ... and it was only with the passage of time, and after I had experienced some horrendous bad luck for being so careless and nonchalant about feng shui, that I began to employ it with any amount of regularity.

When I did, I even started to carry a compass with me wherever I went. For of course the applications and uses of this particular branch of Compass School feng shui is so varied and numerous in scope, I consciously made it one of my success habits !

Sketched here below and on the left is the way the *south* corner of the house was demarcated to determine the location of the master bedroom. The enlargement of the bedroom shows the sleeping direction ...with the head pointed South east. This two major features clinched our descendant's luck for it was only after staying in this room, in this house that we got out baby ! remember though that the directions used here are not universally applicable. Those wishing to activate their descendants luck must first find out what their *nien* yen and *sheng chi* directions are.

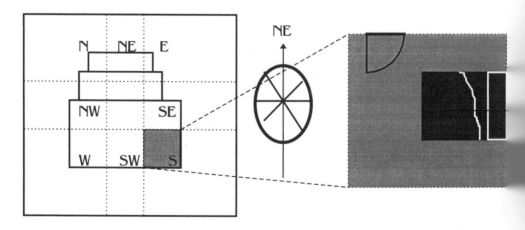

A USEFUL NOTE: *I discovered from the start that although the Chinese place SOUTH at the top when referring to the feng shui compass, as far as application of formulas and everything to do with Chinese feng shui is concerned, any Western type compass can be used.*

Thus when feng shui refers to North, they mean the magnetic North and the Chinese North is similar to the Western North. It is thus not necessary to flip the directions around. The same goes for practice in either the Northern or Southern hemisphere.

There are practitioners whose understanding of the fundamentals of feng shui is not sufficiently deep and who thus advised their clients in the Southern hemisphere that feng shui North was to be read as South, and vice versa. Their rationale was that since South represents the element fire, it must refer to the equator .... This is actually incorrect. The fire element in the South is derived from the Arrangement of Trigrams around the Pa Kua compass. For yang dwellings (ie houses of the living as opposed to houses of the dead ... graveyards) the Later Heaven Arrangement of Trigrams around the Pa Kua applies, and this places the Trigram Li (which means fire) in the South. As such irrespective of where you live, in the North or South hemisphere, the same element symbolism applies.

We still live in the same house, but since those years, I have systematically introduced improvements and feng shui features to ensure continuos family harmony and happiness.

I have become something of an expert in feng shui. When I returned to Malaysia after spending nine years in Hong Kong, I had accumulated a depth of knowledge about its practice and its underlying philosophy. In the process I have come to develop a deep respect for the science.

Feng shui is not difficult to learn but to incorporate it into our living space correctly requires practice.. Feng shui is not static. It is dynamic and fluid. Aspirations do change over time depending on which stage of life we are at. Feng shui can be used to improve every single aspiration of the human condition. It can enhance love, romance and marriage; or it can attract opportunities and improve chances for success; and it can give boring careers a real boost.

Feng shui can attract help and goodwill towards the home, bring helpful people into your life, give you a way out when you get into trouble, and perhaps, most promising of all ... it can make you enormously rich and wealthy.

Feng shui can give you wonderful children, helping the next generation become better focused and better motivated so that exam grades improve and opportunities for scholastic advancement multiply.

Enhancing children's luck

When you consciously address the family aspect of feng shui, you will be creating balance in your life You will find it easier to cope with children problems ‐ anything from health uncertainties to frustration caused by disobedience and unruly behavior.

Good family feng shui fosters closer relationships between parents and offspring; enhances communication and helps ensure they do not get carried away by the excesses of youthful temptations. Where they lack the wisdom to see the dangers, feng shui will help by deflecting bad outcomes ... Children will also study better and become more clearly focused. Exam grades improve and it becomes easier to motivate them.

I used feng shui to help my niece and nephew. I taught them to activate their auspicious corners based on their birth dates. This would ensure general good luck. Next I changed their sitting/study positions, orienting their desks in a way which makes them face their best directions. Next I actively energized their education/study corner. The universal corner to energize to improve grades and exam results is the Northeast corner.

The Trigram represented by this direction is the trigram Ken which is shown here. This trigram represents young children. It also symbolizes the mountain and a time of preparation. The single unbroken yang line above with two broken yin lines below indicates the seed preparing to break through the earth.

Thus the Northeast corner can be energized to assist in the attainment of knowledge to prepare for later life. This corner or trigram is represented by the element earth, and the best way to activate it is to use either natural quartz crystals, or failing that to use man made faceted lead crystals. Place these crystals on a table, and try to make them catch the rays of the morning sun thereby making rainbows.

This will be especially potent. The kind of crystals that can be used are illustrated here ...

> *This is a natural quartz crystal. Place it on a table in the NE corner of the room, or on the NE corner of the desk. Get them from any crystal shop. A small one will do ...*

Man made crystal paperweights, made to resemble gemstones may also be as effective. They are excellent energizers for the study corner; Display them on a table..

Another object which I use throughout the rooms of my home are these hanging faceted crystal balls which can be purchased from any shop that sells crystal ware or crystal chandeliers

Get one or several of these crystals (about one inch in diameter) and hang them in the NE corner of the bedroom or study room. If there is a window in that corner, hang the crystal in that corner to catch the sunlight. The facets of the crystal will break up the light and create beautiful rainbows that bring in precious *yang* energy into the room every morning).

They are particularly effective, and I have lots of these crystals in my home so that every morning, my living room is brought beautifully alive by the stunning rainbows created all round the room.

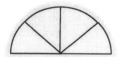

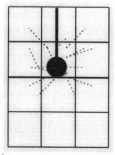

Hang faceted crystals on windows that face the sun, to create beautiful rainbows in your home. This utilizes the light from the sun and brings in valuable yang energy into the home ... it makes for liveliness and activity, and can also represent success and business opportunities ... Do not over do. One crystal per window is sufficient.

If you find crystals too expensive, another method of activating the earth element of the NE is to purchase a globe. This symbolizes *big earth* and is also very effective.

There are many uses for this globe symbol but perhaps the best way of using it is for energizing the knowledge corner of the study desk, or of the bedroom child's.

My niece benefited almost immediately. She had taken her **A** level exams and had done badly. It had devastated her because she had already been admitted into Bristol University but her grades proved woefully inadequate. Instead of the A's and B's she was expecting for her Maths and Economics, she obtained D's and E's. It had been a blow to her ambitions. So she re sat the papers six months later, but this time after activating her knowledge corner. This second time around, she got an **A** for her Maths and **B** for her Economics !

Meanwhile we had also activated the children's corner of my mother's house to benefit the children. This we did by focusing on the West sector of the house. To our dismay we found that this part of the house was where the store room was located, and inside the store room were brooms and mops - not very auspicious!

Brooms and mops in the wrong corners can cause bad luck !!

I did not want the *children luck* of my mother's house swept away, so we removed the brooms and mops and kept them elsewhere. Meanwhile, because the store room was there, it was not much point activating that corner, since there would be an excess of yin energy.

The best thing to do in the circumstances was to focus our attention on the living room where they spent a great deal of their time. First I moved the Television and hi fi equipment so that they were placed against the WEST wall. This is because the West direction is represented by the element *metal*. The wall itself, previously painted in blue was repainted white, once again to symbolize the correct element. Then I hung a wind chime on the ceiling where a protruding corner beam created a certain amount of inauspicious killing breath. And finally I placed a wall clock on the wall next to a landscape painting of undulating mountains and hills.

This tapped into the Productive cycle of the elements where the element earth produces metal. The painting and the wall clock would strengthen the energy of the West wall, thereby activating the children's corner of the living room.

Household objects like electronic equipment... hi fi sets, radios, TV's and computer terminals, as well as wall clocks all represent the metal element and can be placed in the WEST corners to energize what that corner symbolizes which is children luck.

Both my niece and nephew are benefiting from their good feng shui. She has started University and has become focused and motivated, and she is looking forward to going to the US. The boy has buckled down to continuing his education, which had been interrupted, and he too has become focused about his future.

CHAPTER 11
ENHANCING YOUR LOVE LIFE WITH FENG SHUI
Improving marriage luck with feng shui

Some years ago, soon after I had published my first book on feng shui, I bumped into a long forgotten friend in the supermarket, someone I had not seen for many years. She was pregnant, expecting her second child. But far from being happy, she burst into tears when I congratulated her. The poor woman could barely hide her intense unhappiness and I was at a loss to understand. Was there something wrong with the coming of her new baby ? As we stood there between shelves of curry powder and rice packets, two long lost friends, I could feel her embarrassment, and her obvious unhappiness.

Over a cup of tea in a cafe nearby, some time later, the whole story came tumbling out. She was six months pregnant, but she dreaded the coming of the child growing inside her. It turned out that shortly after they had discovered she was pregnant, David her husband, had started coming home late. He had also grown cold and distant, and just three weeks before, they had had a particularly violent quarrel; he had left the house, after slapping her with the full force of a man possessed, and had not returned since then. David had never hit her in all their six years of marriage. She had been appalled at this violent side of her husband, and it seemed like he was not the same man at all ! A successful architect, he had been the most loving of husbands and had been a tower of strength during her first pregnancy. It seemed like her world had suddenly crashed around her.

And then a week ago she had discovered he was living with another woman.

Gaik told me she felt like committing suicide. She blamed herself for getting pregnant, flagellated herself for putting on weight, and was altogether quite absurdly self abusive, blaming her bad temper, her morning sickness and her general moodiness for his leaving her. I told her I thought she was being ridiculous, yet I knew she desperately needed some moral support. So I went home with her and of course being the feng shui busy body that I am, I saw the cause of her problems immediately.

Next to the handsome main door was a beautifully landscaped *koi* pond, *but it was on the right hand side of the door* ! As if that wasn't bad enough, immediately inside the main door they had decorated *the foyer*

146

area in stunning glass tiles, which looked quite beautiful actually, especially with the green plant against it, except that the plant looked half dead, and of course the glass tiles was in reality quite deadly feng shui !

About three feet into the house, two steps led down into the living room and opposite the steps a beautiful bar area had been constructed. The *sharp edge of the bar area pointed ominously at the main door* ! I was appalled at these structures and inquired how long they had lived there.

" *Three years*" she replied, but she admitted they had only recently renovated and redecorated the house. The bar, the pond, the glass tiles were all new !

"*And what about the bedroom*" I asked, " *has that been redecorated as well ?* "

Gaik was quite sheepish by that time, and probably a little put out by my insistence at seeing the bedroom. Less the reader misconstrue my actions, I have to confess that although I do not normally like investigating the feng shui of others, when I do find myself doing it, I believe in being as thorough as possible. In Gaik's case the situation had obviously gone out of hand, and if I was right, perhaps something could indeed be done to repair a previously happy marriage.

As I suspected, the bedroom too had succumbed to the interior decorator's zeal. An entire wall had been fitted with stunning imported mirror tiles ! And a beautiful canopy had been built just above the bed itself. The canopy covered about one fifth of the bed so that it resembled a beam over the sleeping couple ! And to make matters worse, a blue sleeping light had been fitted under the bed itself to *add to the atmosphere* !

Gaik and her husband was not to know of course that the entire tableaux had created an excess of yin energy which was to prove extremely harmful.

What puzzled me when I saw the bedroom was how on earth Gaik had got pregnant in such a overly yin bedroom !

With such bad feng shui, I could not see how such an auspicious occurrence had taken place. When I voiced my puzzlement to her, she told me they had actually moved out while the house was being renovated, and had only moved back just after Gaik had discovered she was pregnant.

" *You mean you moved house while in the family way*" I asked surprised, because I simply assumed everyone knew that during a time of pregnancy one should really not move house. Miserably she nodded.

Oh dear, I thought, how do I tell her to do what needs to be done. I am never in favor of there being any knocking and hammering in any house that is occupied by an expectant mother.

I decided to take the risk anyway and immediately told her to do the following:

In the living area:
1. Immediately cover the fish pond (marked A in the sketch). "*Give the Japanese carp away*" I advised and close up the pond. When she protested that David would hit the roof I reminded her that he was no longer around to protest ! Having a pond on the right hand side of the main door usually cause the man of the house to take up with another woman.

2. Close up the wall with the glass tiles with a plywood wall and either paint it or put some wallpaper to camouflage the wood (marked B in the sketch) . The glass tiles resembled mirrors and reflecting the main door caused any good luck *chi* that entered the home to fly right out again !

3. As for the bar I told her to place a large plant to block off the sharp edge that was pointed directly at the door (marked C in the sketch) . Also to place a plant at place marked D.

In the bedroom:
4. I told her to immediately dismantle the half canopy over the bed. Sleeping under the canopy was quite inauspicious and would cause her to go out of her mind with worry. (Marked E). This is because the canopy represents a burden above her, and as her canopy was a dark shade of blue it could also represent a cloud ... not at all auspicious ... she would be better off without it.

5. Next I told her to change the blue light under the bed to red, or better still do away with it altogether.

6. Finally I strongly advised her to throw out the deadly mirror tiles facing her bed. (Marked F). Mirrors in front of the bed were bad enough but mirror tiles were worst. They distort the images reflected, thereby causing severe imbalance. <u>Here are the diagrams to illustrate</u> :

<u>The living room area:</u>

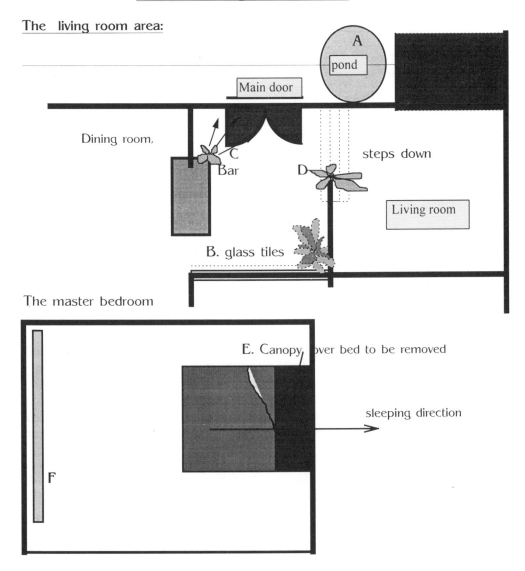

The master bedroom

Then we examined her auspicious directions and based on her date of birth I discovered that her *nien yen* direction, which influenced her family and marriage happiness was actually east.

She had been sleeping in a direction which represented one of her worse directions i.e. west. Gaik was an <u>East group person</u> and so was her husband. The redecorated bedroom had placed the bed in a way which made them both sleep in their inauspicious *six killings* direction ! The change was actually easily achieved because all it required was for the bed to be moved and re oriented to the other side of the room.

It took Gaik less than a week to make the changes suggested, and David returned home soon after. He did not immediately become loving again, but he did apologize in the sort of way men do, which was not much of an apology, but Gaik was so relieved she refrained from asking about the other woman.

She herself was feeling better and stronger, and as the months passed and baby Sharon was born, David did finally become once again the family man he always had been. Perhaps it was a coincidence that things improved after the feng shui changes although I don't believe so.

In Gaik and David's case, the bad marriage feng shui had caused him to be unlucky, thereby allowing him to be caught by a predatory female when he had stopped by a bar with some developer clients of his. The bar girl in question had used some dirty potion to snare him. All of this was to come out later when Gaik's mother investigated the temporary aberration of her son in law. She soon arranged to have him cured.

Less you readers jump to the conclusion that the potency of good feng shui works by overcoming spells and that sort of thing, I should hasten to say that this is not the case. Feng shui creates either harmonious or unbalanced flows of chi which in turn cause good luck or bad luck. When bad luck enters a marriage, either party can become influenced by others or worse, as in David's case succumb to unscrupulous people.

Feng shui is thus not just for making you wealthy or successful or rich. More important, it creates harmony and happiness in the household. Thus for those just beginning to get interested in this ancient Chinese method of creating a balanced environment and living space, start your practice and investigation by taking a defensive attitude. Take a second look at your main door and your sleeping environment.

Deflect all edges, beams and protruding corners that seem to be pointed at either the door or at the bed. These *poison arrows* cause the most havoc, and should be deflected or diffused

SHARING A FABULOUS FENG SHUI TIP

Many years ago a FENG SHUI Master in Hong Kong told me about the balancing method of activating the SOUTHWEST to ignite romance in one's life ... I have since passed this on to quite a number of my girlfriends, and in almost every instance their social and love life improved tremendously. There were those also who had had problems getting the men in their life to make a commitment, and after energizing their marriage corner with this method soon found themselves being proposed to ...

The method

Buy a crystal bowl (earth); place some coloured glass stones, or coloured marbles in the bowl earth) Or some steel pebbles (metal); pour in some water (water). Float some tiny flowers on the water (wood) and finally place a candle in the center of the bowl and light it (fire). This creates <u>a balance of the five elements with earth dominating</u> and it apparently does wonders in activating the marriage corner.

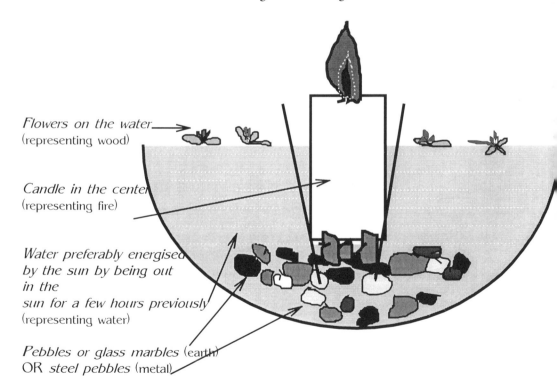

Flowers on the water
(representing wood)

Candle in the center
(representing fire)

Water preferably energised
by the sun by being out
in the
sun for a few hours previously
(representing water)

Pebbles or glass marbles (earth)
OR *steel pebbles* (metal)

Crystal bowl (representing earth)

Can feng shui jazz up your social life ?

Can romance and marriage really be made sweeter with feng shui ? Can this thousand year old science jazz up your love life, rekindle the faded embers of a marriage gone sour, or even, bring you the man of your dreams ? Less I am accused of getting carried away and becoming too extravagant in raising your expectations, let me say that I have personally seen feng shui work again and again in this important sector of life, sometimes in ways that surprise me ... let me tell you the story of Nancy, my beautiful interior decorator girlfriend who was my special chum during my years in Hong Kong.

Nancy, a single mother, was both vivacious and attractive. Originally from Singapore, she and her first husband had divorced in Hong Kong where they had lived because of his work. Nancy had picked up the pieces of her life after the divorce, building her own decoration business and bringing up two beautiful children. For well over ten years, her business flourished and she achieved financial independence. The one thing she wanted most of all - to find someone kind and strong and wonderful to share her life - eluded her. Despite brief engagements and near misses, Nancy remained frustratingly single ! Until we discovered why.

Her Mid levels apartment, beautifully decorated as only a home belonging to someone in her profession can be, was laid out in a way which sent *six killings chi* to her marriage chances day after day !
An elaborate toilet/cum bathroom was located smack in the marriage corner of her apartment - the Southwest ! The Southwest coincided with her <u>personal</u> *nien yen* or marriage direction ! The toilet was flushing her marriage chances down the loo ! Because the Southwest was doubly significant in her case, the effect had been quite potent !

Toilets flush away romance/marriage prospects if located in the marriage corner of the room/apartment or home. Homes with children of marriageable age should <u>not</u> have this particular feature; otherwise marriage prospects and happiness for *all* the children get dimmed. If you have this feature in your home, it is best to reduce the use of it, or better yet, close it up altogether. Indeed it is better to have small toilets than large luxurious bathrooms. And keep toilets closed.

I advised Nancy to relocate the toilet, and to instead put all the symbols of conjugal bliss and romance in the SOUTHWEST corner of her apartment. Nancy went to work with a vengeance. The contractors were brought in, and Nancy herself got a list of things that could represent good marriage luck from me and then went shopping. She was determined to get all the suitable feng shui *activators* to be placed in this all important corner.

Nancy is not a person who does things by half, so that by the time she was finished implementing all my suggestions, the Southwest corner of her apartment, which was located next to her bedroom looked delightfully romantic.

She bought Chinese love knots, which she hung on the walls, had her favorite calligrapher write out the double happiness word (which signifies marriage), and this she cleverly converted into a table top placed under glass; she bought wooden carvings of mandarin ducks which she displayed under the coffee table in a corner and she hung a beautiful painting of the *mou tan* flower (the peony, although roses will do just as well.) on the wall.

The Double happiness symbol   Mandarin ducks

Chinese love knot   Symbol of flower

Three months after making these changes, Nancy met Ray at a dinner party, and a year later they married. The last I heard, Nancy and Ray had left Hong Kong and are now living in blissful retirement in the suburbs of Sydney, Australia. Those of you keen on adding some sparkle into your love life and enhancing your marriage prospects can try to do exactly what Nancy did.

First identify the Southwest corner of your home/ apartment of room. The Southwest corner represents the marriage and family corner under the Black Hat School of Feng Shui. If you succeed in activating this corner, it will vastly improve your marriage and love feng shui.

In addition, you can also investigate your <u>personal marriage corner</u>, i.e. one that is based on your date of birth. To do this, determine the lunar year of your birth which generally corresponds to the western calendar except that you must make adjustments for the Chinese date of your particular year of birth. Then use this formula to determine your KUA number:

The formula for Women
1. Take the year of your birth
2. Add the last two digits
3. Reduce to a single number
4. Add 5. The answer is your KUA number

EXAMPLE: YEAR OF BIRTH 1945
4+5=9; 9+5=14; 1+4=5   So the KUA number is 5
EXAMPLE YEAR OF BIRTH 1977
7+7=14: 1+4=5; 5+5=10=1. So the KUA number is 1.

The formula for Men
1.   Take the year of your birth
2.   Add the last two digits
3.   Reduce to a single number
4.   Deduct from 10. The answer is your KUA number

EXAMPLE: YEAR OF BIRTH say 1936
3+6=9; and 10-9=1
So the KUA number is 1
EXAMPLE: YEAR OF BIRTH say 1948
4=8+12; 1+2 +3
10-3=7   So the KUA number is 7

Based on your KUA number, the following will be the corresponding marriage/romance corners to also activate:

Kua number 1, the marriage corner is South
Kua number 3, the marriage corner is Southeast
Kua number 4, the marriage corner is East
Kua number 9, the marriage corner is North
Kua number 5, the marriage corner is West
Kua number 2, the marriage corner is Northwest
Kua number 6, the marriage corner is Southwest
Kua number 7, the marriage corner is Northeast
Kua number 8, the marriage corner is West

Once you know your personal marriage corner, try to make sure neither the toilet, nor the kitchen nor the storeroom is situated there. These press down on the marriage luck ! Also make certain you do not put things like brooms and mops in this corner !

Instead, use your imagination to activate the corner by placing symbols of conjugal bliss in this corner. Use your imagination ... e.g. if you cannot find mandarin ducks, use budgerigars (or western love birds !). If you cannot find a painting of a peony, how about a wedding bouquet ?

A pair of love birds

Wedding bouquet

Just make sure that you hang everything in a pair to signify two people rather than one ! Do not be like another friend of mine, who put the picture of a bride in her marriage corner without the groom. It did not work !

For those of you who are already married, here is a tip I picked up during one of my tours of the Forbidden City Palaces in Beijing. Deep in the heart of the Complex where the emperors were entertained by his concubines, my attention was drawn to the lavish use of the double happiness symbol which was carved onto beds and screens and dividers. And in front of the conjugal bed was a beautifully embroidered silk curtain which had been decorated with a hundred little children – to signify many descendants ! For those wanting children it is thus a good idea to hang paintings of small children in full view of the bed !

Here are also two important tips on what to avoid. I was told by many feng shui experts that these two taboos must be strenuously observed.

I. Do not sleep with mirrors directly facing the bed. Apart from being generally bad feng shui, mirrors in the bedroom also cause quarrels between husband and wife; they also encourage one of the partners to be unfaithful, or a third party will cause trouble for the couple. No matter how beautiful the mirrors look, please throw them out ! And while we are on the subject of mirrors, full length mirrors are bad, but mirror tiles are worse ! They represent knives and poison arrows in the bedroom.

2. Do not have water on the right hand side of the main door.

From the inside looking out, make sure that any pond, aquarium, fountain or painting of water is placed on the left hand side. If it is on the right hand side of the main door, it might bring success or wealth luck, but your husband will have a tendency to stray, to have girlfriends outside. In short, he will be unfaithful, and if your luck is low, he could even leave you.

I have often been asked about the origins of this particular taboo, and I can only surmise that in the old days when feng shui was practiced by the upper classes of Chinese society, it was seldom the women who arranged for feng shui consultations.

In the days of the emperor's court, feng shui expertise was regarded as an important part of affairs of state.

In those days too, from the emperor down, all successful and important officials had concubines. The higher and more important the rank, the larger the number of secondary wives and concubines.

Water has always been acknowledged as a symbol of material success, and features widely in the practice of feng shui. Thus placing water to bring success also implies hoping for a whole harem of wives ! Thus the exact placement of water becomes important to women of this century when polygamy is no longer as widely accepted or condoned.

Can feng shui help you find a soul mate ... ?

Not only can feng shui activate social life, mend a fast breaking marriage and improve family happiness, it can also be used to improve marriage opportunities. Time and again I have seen it work wonders for girlfriends of mine, who, fed up with their love relationships going nowhere, turned to feng shui for help. Or hapless mothers wringing their hands in despair as they watch their daughters' relationships flounder and break up even as they advanced along in years, no husband, and thus no prospective son in law in sight ... oh dear !

I remember several years ago, I was invited for tea to the home of an old friend whom I shall call Datin Theresa. She was a contemporary of mine, and had worked briefly as a teacher before retiring to look after her three children. Her husband, a prominent property developer, had urged her to stop work to concentrate on the children, and indeed this lovely lady did a brilliant job.

Her two girls, Marianne and Priscilla grew up into beautiful and talented young women, while John the son became a handsome six footer. All three children are very warm, sociable and successful young professionals with sparkling personalities. They were not short of suitors !

But Marianne was thirty two, John thirty and Priscilla twenty five when I visited their home that lazy Sunday. Datin Theresa confided in me that she often wondered why all three of her children were having such a hard time finding life partners.

" *Look at Marianne,* " she said to me " *she is a lovely young woman ... and she has so many boyfriends ... but she is already past thirty and still there is no one serious ... and as for John, he doesn't lack for girlfriends ... but like the sister, he doesn't seem to be interested in anyone ... and as for Priscilla, she doesn't even seem to like boys at all ...".*

Then she had leaned over and said, " *Do you think there is something wrong with the feng shui of our house ..."*

I knew what was going through her mind. Datin Theresa and her family lived in a large sprawling home in Damansara Heights. Her husband's business was going well. The family enjoyed a great relationship, and to all intents and purposes, everything seemed to be going well.
"Not that I believe in feng shui," she added, as an afterthought, *"but surely our feng shui must be quite good ... so why are the children still single ... why am I having such a hard time becoming a grandmother"*

It was obvious from the tone of her voice this was a sore point. I knew she had invited me round to check out her feng shui and as I gazed out at the beautiful lawn in front of us, at the large swimming pool by the side of the patio and at the lavish furnishings around us, I could not see anything seriously wrong with her feng shui at all. Like she said, the family was prosperous and she had a great family life. Her husband was faithful to her, they were respectable members of the community and they all enjoyed good health ...

Datin Theresa and her husband both belonged to the East group and were thus very well suited for each other ... their lucky directions were *southeast, east, north and south* and they were very compatible. I brought out my tiny traveling compass to get my bearings and discovered that happily for them, their front door faced South East, an excellent direction for both of them, in fact the best ... When I checked the directions of Marianne, John and Priscilla, it was a different stroty.

I discovered they were all West group people although their respective *nien yen* or family directions were different. This meant that the auspicious direction of the main door did nothing for them. As long as they were still kids, the parents' good fortune directions reflected on them as well, but as they grew up and started working it was another story. Generally however since according to the Chinese view of things one did not really become an adult until one was married, all three children continued to benefit from the parent's good feng shui.

On personal matters however it was something else again ! I discovered when I went on a small tour of their large house, that all the toilets in the home were located in places and corners that were highly damaging to the children's marriage prospects. To start with the guest toilet (which was also the most frequently used toilet) was located in the Southwest corner of the home.

The Southwest is regarded as the universal marriage corner and having a frequently used toilet located there makes for very bad marriage luck indeed ! This usually has the effect of flushing marriage prospects down the loo !

To make matters worse, Marianne, the eldest girl's bedroom was located in her worst *chueh ming* or total loss position and the attached toilet in her bedroom suite was placed exactly in her personal *nien yen* or marriage/family corner. As for John, the kitchen of the house was located in his *nien yen* corner !

Toilets and kitchens when placed in locations that represent auspicious fortune cause the good fortune to be pressed down.

In Marianne and John's case their family luck was affected, thereby spoiling their chances of finding spouses ... Priscilla's feng shui was the worse of the three since every one of her relevant doorways and rooms corresponded to her worst directions. Her bedroom was located in her *six killings* direction while her head was pointed also to this most inauspicious direction while she slept.

Her room had been painted in shades of baby blue and above her bed was an abstract painting which depicted three women. The bedroom was entirely too *yin* by far ... Of the three Priscilla had started out being the most promising. She had gained brilliant results for her O levels in the UK but by the time she entered University she had started keeping company with another woman, moving out of the family flat in London, and dropping out of University ...

158

These developments proved a nightmare to the parents ... and by the time she reached her twenty fifth birthday, her gay relationship with her woman friend had created a permanent rift with her parents. All of which made for some pretty heartbreaking moments ... so was it a certain amount of unbalanced feng shui that had caused Theresa's problems with her children ?

I advised her on the various methods of activating her children's corners, and energizing the marriage prospects for both Marianne and John. The situation called for them to move into two other rooms in the house which had been set aside as guest rooms. I also told her to place a huge boulder tied with a red ribbon in the Southwest corner of her garden, as well as a crystal chandelier in the Southwest corner of her living room.

Feng shui or not, Marianne is now married to a doctor and she has given her mum two delightful grandchildren, while John too has found himself a perfectly nice girl and was married last year ! As for Priscilla, she had moved out of the house and today continues to live with her friend. But the parents have accepted the situation.

I dislike drawing simplified conclusions as to the efficacy of feng shui at work but when I see happy developments like this I cannot help feeling a certain satisfaction that when one least expects it, feng shui can indeed create a certain amount of happiness ...

Richard and Lyn find love within three months ...

Take the case of two young people who befriended me through my daughter ... in the summer of 1995, Jennifer met a very nice young man riding at the Polo Club.

He was rich, good looking and extremely eligible. We soon became family friends and one day Richard confided in me that he was already 32 years old and still seemed to be having trouble finding someone really suitable to marry. He was ready for marriage, he said but somehow it seemed terrifically difficult finding someone ... indeed he had only just broken off with his girlfriend.

One day he was at my home and we sat down to talk seriously about feng shui. I gave him a one hour lesson and presented him with all my books, on the condition that he devote some time to read them, and if possible to put some of the tips contained in my books to work.

Richard lived in Penang, and true to his word he went back and immediately set about applying some of the principles contained in my various volumes.

Meanwhile, because he was such a nice young man, we, my daughter and I, decided to introduce him to a lovely young lady, who at 28 also seemed to be having difficult finding someone suitable. Lynn too wanted marriage and babies.

The introduction fell rather flat as both seemed distinctly cool with each other. They got along well but any hopes we had of them becoming romantically attached seemed doomed to failure.

The weeks passed, and in January, Richard met another girl who caught his fancy. He came skiing with us to Vail in the USA and on the chair lift up one of the runs, we sat together. I asked him how he felt about Lyn, and he seemed vague about his feelings, but I got the impression that he was not that interested. When I returned, Lyn called me and confided that she really liked Richard, and what was she to do ...

Let him know I said matter of factly . Then I added, *Perhaps you should move out of your present house. Get a flat of your own and then activate the marriage corner of the flat. Perhaps your family house is not so conducive to your marriage prospects* ...

Lyn actually found a flat to rent the very next day. Located five minutes from her mum's house in Bukit Tunku, it was a perfect bachelor girl's pad. Next she called Richard and invited him to help her move in ...

Well, to cut a long story short, they fell in love soon after and within a few months they were married !

Richard later informed me that he had indeed activated his marriage corner, and it had taken him exactly 60 days for it to work !

Lyn and Richard are their real names and today they are blissfully and happily in love with each other and they are legally married although the wedding dinner will not be until the following year. I had told them that this year of the fire rat was not very auspicious for getting married, that the year of the ox was better.

Since they could not wait to tie the knot they have registered and I will have to wait until next year to eat the roast pig that is traditionally served to the person who introduces the bride and groom.

So can feng shui be used to lend a helping hand to those of you having a hard time finding a soul mate, the answer is yes. Just activate your Southwest corner, and if possible also activate your *nien yen* corner. Then wait and see what happens. Remember that the SOUTHWEST is of the earth element and anything made of earth is suitable ie a crystal, lights (as fire produces earth); or even symbolic marriage tokens ...

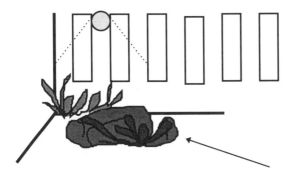

To activate your marriage corner, identify the SOUTHWEST corner of your garden, then place a boulder tied with red ribbon there. This activates the element of that corner effectively. If you like you can also place a garden light in that corner. This is a really effective method !!

A feng shui tip for finding your soul mate

It is necessary to understand that in the practice of feng shui the five element theory is extremely important when it comes to activating the relevant corners.

Each of the eight corners that correspond to the compass directions are said to symbolize a particular life aspiration, and the Southwest, being the place of the trigram KUN ie three broken lines as shown here, represents *mother earth.*

Thus to activate this corner, the earth element becomes extremely important, especially since this is also the corner of big earth. In the cycle of relationships, earth is produced by fire. So the fire element also becomes important for energizing this corner ....

One very easy way of activating this corner in the garden is thus to combine the five element theory with that of the channeling method. This is illustrated here. It is a very effective method, and unless you are ready for marriage , it is better NOT to try it !!

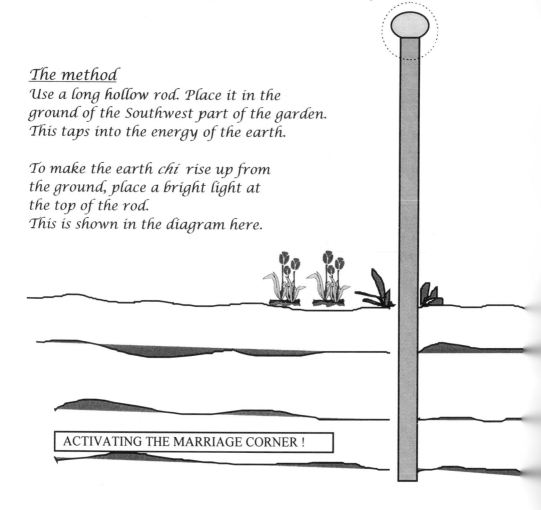

The method
Use a long hollow rod. Place it in the ground of the Southwest part of the garden. This taps into the energy of the earth.

To make the earth *chi* rise up from the ground, place a bright light at the top of the rod. This is shown in the diagram here.

ACTIVATING THE MARRIAGE CORNER !

CHAPTER TWELVE
ACTIVATING DRAGONS & TIGERS

A cousin of mine once called on me to check out his recently renovated home. Since adding an additional level to his single level bungalow in Petaling Jaya, a suburb of Kuala Lumpur, Jonathan's family had been plagued by illness. His two children came down with a bad case of asthma, his wife, Chan began complaining of serious backache problems, and his mother in law had recently been diagnosed as suffering from diabetes. He wondered whether all these ailments could be due to the new level of rooms which had been added. Jonathan himself was always feeling drained and listless. He seemed to tire easily and seemed to have to drag himself out of bed each morning where before he had been full of energy.

He was convinced that something was definitely wrong. In recent weeks he and Chan had started becoming extremely intolerant of each other. At first he had attributed it to the heat wave they were experiencing from the hot dry weather but when temperatures cooled with the coming of the rainy season and still things did not improve, he began suspecting that his family's recent travails could well be a feng shui problem.

It was a good thing he asked me actually because when I went to see his house, I discovered that in addition to building a new level to his home, Jonathan had also created a small wading pool on the right hand side of his garden. The small pool was meant for his children, and he had intended to convert it into a fish pond when they grew older ... and to make the pool look nicer, he had also installed a pump which created a very pretty fountain. The fountain and pool made his home look very nice indeed.

The right hand side of his garden also corresponded to the West side of his compound, so in effect the pond was placed in the corner that is represented by the metal element. In the five element cycle of relationships, metal produces water ... thus the pond (signifying water) was exhausting the metal ! This created an excess of tired listless energy which overflowed into the home ...

But worse still was that in having the fountain, Jonathan had unknowingly activated the *white tiger* ! In feng shui the *green dragon* is generally deemed to be the left side of the front door and the white tiger is on the right hand side ... and the east is regarded as the dragon side while the west side is the tiger side.

The dragon side brings wealth and prosperity and good health when it is properly activated. But the tiger side should always be left alone. The tiger must not be disturbed or activated, as activating the tiger usually has the effect of having the tiger turn against the residents, bringing ill luck which often initially manifests in the form of illness ...

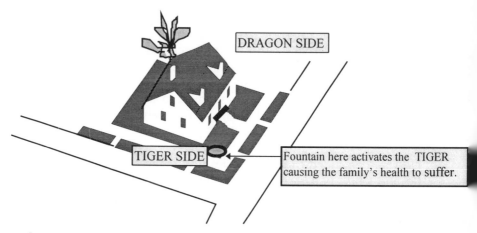

DRAGON SIDE

TIGER SIDE

Fountain here activates the TIGER causing the family's health to suffer.

I advised Jonathan to have the pond covered up, and he was definitely to do away with the fountain. If he wanted a pond or any other water feature, I said, it would be far advisable to locate it on the left side of the garden ... the dragon side, and even better to apply the water compass formula method. Although the calculations and measuring process would seem tedious, it would be well worth the effort. If he was too lazy however, he could always play safe and put the pond in the North part of the compound, as this corresponded to the water element.

Jonathan immediately implemented my suggestion, relieved that the offending feng shui structure or feature had nothing to do with the additional level of rooms. Once the pond had been covered, the children recovered. His wife's problems with back aches were much reduced and the old lady's diabetes responded to medication.

In fact the family's energy levels revived and Jonathan henceforth became a firm believer of feng shui. He actually went on to build his water dragon according to my book on Water Feng Shui. Coincidence or not, Jonathan was promoted soon after the installation of his water dragon, and today he is a divisional general manager in his company. Chan meanwhile has started her own interior decoration business which is flourishing ...

Activating the white tiger

This is one of the more common causes of feng shui problems that can wreak havoc on a home. Bad luck can sometimes come in the form of sickness, but this is usually only the start of bad luck. Sometimes the consequences can be so severe as to cause death for one of the residents. Or it can cause the family's wealth luck to take a turn for the worse.

Activating the white tiger is a big taboo in feng shui, and usually, experienced feng shui masters make certain that this never happens. For this reason a physical investigation of the site is usually necessary, since a paper drawing cannot adequately describe the contours and characteristics of the surrounding terrain. Thus the way a house is orientated and the placement of the main door plays a vitally important role in establishing good feng shui.

The surrounding hills and terrain have to be *tapped* in such a way that the front door does not confront the tiger hills. The tiger must also NOT be activated or disturbed. But before all of this can be undertaken, it is first necessary to learn to recognize the white tiger.

The white tiger of feng shui can be recognized in one of two ways.

Inside looking out

Firstly, land to the right hand side of the main front door (inside looking out) is usually deemed to be the white tiger. This is when the overall terrain is relatively flat, or if the house in question is located in town or a suburban residential area where there are no hills. Secondly, land on the right side should be slightly lower than land on the left side. The sketch above encompasses both criteria.

165

If we go according to compass directions, it is the west side of any plot that is deemed to be the abode of the white tiger. The east is where the dragon is located.

This corresponds to the classical green dragon, white tiger configuration of classical form school feng shui. According to this description of green dragon white tiger formation, the tiger hills should be slightly lower than the dragon hills. Thus if you use the compass to identify the white tiger these two facts will assist in recognizing the white tiger ...

Problems arise when the right hand side of the land (which is considered the tiger) is HIGHER than the left hand side. How can it be the tiger when it is higher than the so called dragon hills ? See sketch below.

This sort of configuration is regarded as bad feng shui because the Tiger is said then to have overcome the auspicious Dragon. In this case the Tiger has been naturally activated and the home or homes within its vicinity will suffer from bad feng shui, usually manifested in sickness and bad luck. The best way of handling this sort of problem is to install a very bright high light on the dragon side, as shown.

What if the land on the right hand side (said to be the tiger) is higher, BUT corresponds to the East direction according to the Compass ? Does this transform it then into the green dragon ? The answer is YES. Thus if the land on the right hand side of your land is the East corner of your garden it is not considered to be the tiger. The white tiger is now considered to be the land on the west side, in this case even when it is located on the left hand side of the land ! In such a case the configuration of the terrain is regarded as auspicious for the house !

Once you become adept at recognizing the corner of your garden which corresponds to the tiger, you must strenuously avoid doing anything, building any structure or introducing any feature which can be interpreted as activating this potentially ferocious animal. When the tiger comes alive and turns its ferocity on the residents, it creates very bad feng shui indeed !

Usually the tiger is activated when movement or excessive noise is created. Hence fountains, bells, bright lights erected in the place of the white tiger could well be regarded as inauspicious. It is therefore advisable to be alert to inadvertently making these mistakes.

In this context, it should also be mentioned that care be taken to ensure that no paintings of tigers are displayed INSIDE the home, and especially on the west wall. This could well have the effect of activating the tiger, causing it to turn on the residents instead of protecting them.

Paintings of tigers inside the home could well cause illness, and even fatal sickness to befall residents, especially if their horoscope indicates birth years that correspond to small animals (e.g. sheep, rabbit, rooster etc.). It is worse if the tiger depicted is that of a hungry, open mouthed tiger.

The only people who could sustain the presence of tigers inside the home are people born in either tiger or dragon years, since the spirit of the tiger is then regarded to be in synchronization with the resident.

On the other hand tiger paintings hung outside the house, looking out and seemingly on guard at the front door is said to give protection and security to the house hold.

Knowing when something is wrong

I have often been asked how anyone can know if they are suffering from bad feng shui. How do you know that something could be wrong or not quite right with your living space ... and my answer has always been, *try to live in a state of awareness of your environment.*

Especially when you have just moved office or have just started living in a new apartment, room or house. Start by developing a sensitivity to your health. If after you have just moved, you feel yourself being constantly tired; or if every resident living there take turns getting sick ... if you feel listless, out of sorts and forever tired, then something could well be either blocking the flow of good *chi* into your abode; or worse, sending killing energies in your way ...

A great deal of the Chinese definition of luck has to do with enjoying good health and living a long and fruitful life. Longevity is regarded as a premier blessing, for indeed only the truly lucky will have the good fortune to live to a ripe old age, and of being alive to see, and enjoy the successes of their descendants; playing with grandchildren, and generally enjoying the fruits of their labor.

Thus feng shui lays stress on health. Thus also, bad feng shui cause illness which sometimes become fatal when the intangible forces of *the killing breath* created becomes too powerful. Sometimes the problem is easily diagnosed, yet can be tough to deal with, as in the case of a neighbor of mine.

Mrs Yit-Lin Taylor and her family had moved into the apartment directly below mine during the days when I lived in a luxury apartment block on Peak road in Hong Kong. She was married to an English banker and they had recently been transferred to Hong Kong from Tokyo where her husband had worked over the past several years. From the first week of their arrival, and then all through the first six months, they took turns getting sick. Her three small children were always going in and out of hospitals, and finally she too succumbed to some mysterious bug she had picked up on a weekend visit to Bangkok with her husband.

According to her, that was when she decided to listen to some friendly advice from relatives and friends and consulted the feng shui man. This expert was brought in to check out their spacious apartment.

That was how she discovered that terrible *shar chi* was being sent inside her home by the massive round building which dominated the skyline in front of the apartment block. The imposing circular edifice looked like a gigantic joss stick, and its presence so near to us did not augur well for her family's feng shui luck, or for anyone of the other residents staying there, for that matter,

As an aside, although I did not investigate the others, I have to confess that I too suffered bad feng shui from this same round building, but that is another story. The feng shui man installed several mirrors and Pa Kuas, the eight sided octagonal symbol that is decorated with trigrams around it, to ward off the killling *chi* ... the feng shui cure worked, but only for a while, and in the end, they moved out.

This is because the massive building was too powerful, and small mirrors and Pa Kua symbols were really no match at all.

In my neighbor's case the bad feng shui was quite easily diagnosed. Sometimes however sickness caused by inauspicious feng shui may not be due to visible structures. Indeed, quite often, the symptoms of ill health can well be due to the intangible forces caused by the *flying stars* in what is named *fey sin feng shui* . This is the *Lo Shu* numerology based feng shui formula that is widely practiced in Hong Kong. According to this formula, the flying stars are the numbers that fly around the Lo Shu grid, which in turn represents sections of the home.

These numbers, or combinations of numbers, from one to nine, have auspicious and inauspicious meanings, and over time, they change places ie *fly* around the grid in a pattern determined by the formula. This method of feng shui thus addresses the effect which time has on feng shui. It would be easy to apply this formula if the flying sequences were confined to merely a single variable. In *fey sin feng shui* however this is not the case. Indeed the numbers fly differently depending on the week, month, year or twenty year cycle of the Chinese calendar.

And when the star numbers 5 or 2 occur simultaneously in any room, it adversely affects the health of the occupant of the room. Worse, if these same numbers occur simultaneously in the sector of the home or office where the main door is located then everyone in the house will suffer ill health, and sometimes the illness can be fatal.

In Hong Kong, feng shui experts of this particular school, enjoy a roaring trade calculating the *fey sin* numbers of offices and homes of wealthy clients at the start of each lunar new year.

I have written a book on *fey sin feng shui* (entitled Chinese Numerology in feng shui) where star numbers of house sectors have been calculated for each of the years to the year 2000. By superimposing the Lo Shu grid onto your home or office,   you will be able to identify which sections of the home or the office will suffer from bad feng shui in a particular month, or year, thereby avoiding those rooms for that period of bad luck. In the same way you can also identify the auspicious rooms caused by these *fey sin* numbers.

ANOTHER METHOD ...

Longevity and health are also represented by the EAST corners of any room, home or office according to another school of Compass feng shui. This is because the East is symbolized by the trigram Chen, which has a single strong unbroken line below two broken yin lines.

This Trigram suggests the luxuriant growth of Spring that covers the earth with a garment of plants. Thus the element

The trigram Chen   represented is that of big wood.

Wood is the only element amongst the five elements, that is alive and has the capacity to grow. Wood always symbolizes growth, and for a home to enjoy good health, with residents full of energy and vitality, experts of this school of feng shui always advocate that the East sectors of a home are properly activated. This can be done by displaying strong healthy green or flowering plants in the East rooms of the home and in the East corners of the living room.

I have always made sure that the east rooms and corners of my home are *alive* and properly energized by various plants. For feng shui purposes I select only the plants that are easy to care for, and since I live in the tropics, I use only tropical plants which thrive on the hot and humid climate of Malaysia. Perhaps that is why my husband and I, as well as our daughter enjoy reasonably good health, and we deem ourselves extremely lucky to be able to enjoy all sorts of strenuous exercises like horse riding and skiing.

I strenuously avoid prickly plants ... thus cactus shrubs are out. I also avoid stunted plants like *bonsai* no matter how much I admire these miniaturized plants. Instead I go for the succulent jade plant and the succulent cactus that have no thorns. The Chinese look on these as *money plants*, and they are thus doubly auspicious.

For outdoors, in the garden, it is a good idea to plant a clump of bamboo, or have a pine tree in the East corner of your garden since these two plants are traditional symbols of longevity. If there is also a small fountain nearby to symbolize the continuos supply of water (which produces wood in the cycle of elements) it will be even more auspicious.

A clump of bamboos in the east garden is excellent for energizing longevity luck ....

Various varieties of pine trees are also excellent for health luck when placed in the East

Generally trees with good foliage and broad leaves, like ficus tree, are excellent feng shui.

Indoor plants can be either real or artificial, but they should not be dried or dead ! It is better to display artificial plants than dead or dying plants. Remember that dead plants emanate *shar chi* and causes the energy to become excessively *yin* in a corner (the east) which should ideally be *yang* !

Good health cannot possibly be suggested by dying or unhealthy plants. So those of you career people who are too busy to care for your plants, I strongly suggest that you go for the beautiful artificial plants that are so freely available in supermarkets and flower shops. Displaying flowers instead of green plants is just as effective. Plants and flowers like these are acceptable ...

But do do avoid plants like these INSIDE the home. The are bad for your health ! They are also inauspicious.

The reason is surely obvious. These are plants that have thorns and pointed needles which create *shar chi* or *killing breath*. A hotel owner I know did not believe me when I told him that the two big cactus plants he had placed just inside the entrance of his hotel's Mexican restaurant was bad feng shui. He could not understand why the restaurant simply had no customers despite having been beautifully done up and serving some of the nicest nachos and margaritas around town ...

Finally, after about four months, he decided to remove the offending cactus plants, which was of course sending out *shar chi* to the entrance thereby definitely not encouraging business ... and as soon as he did that business started to pick up. Soon his restaurant had built up a loyal following and through word of mouth the business grew.

He also very quickly had the two large landscaped pots of cactus placed just inside the lobby of his small hotel removed as well ...

ACAPULCO ... RESTAURANT

Cactus plants inside the restaurant drives away the customers

The trigram CHIEN attracts mentors

Probably the strongest and most important trigram, in terms of meanings associated with it is the trigram CHIEN which variously symbolizes heaven, the father, the patriarch, the elder statesman, the leader ... In the placement of trigrams around the Pa Kua, CHIEN is placed in the South in the Early Heaven Arrangement. This is the trigram arrangement which is used in the Pa Kua when it is used as a cure or antidote against poison arrows, or to combat other forms of *shar chi*. This arrangement of the trigrams, with CHIEN above is also used when investigating and analyzing the feng shui of *yin* dwellings, ie. when designing the orientation of grave sites for the burial of ancestors.

 The trigram CHIEN

In *yang* feng shui, the Pa Kua arrangement according to the Later Heaven placement is used and this puts CHIEN in the Northwest. And arising from this all feng shui experts point to the NW as the direction from which mentors and leaders, patriarchs and advisors luck emanates. If you want help from a higher authority; if you wish to enjoy the goodwill of some powerful person, it is the NORTHWEST corner of your home which needs to be activated, and because the ruling element here is big metal, it is things metal or things which produce metal which can be used really effectively here.

Personally I have found that the most easily available symbols of the Northwest are either windchimes or bells. Gold coloured chimes and bells are very effective. This was the method used by my woman friend who got elevated to such high positions I am so tempted to tell you who she is but she has made me promise not to reveal her name. Indeed for years, everyone speculated how she seemed to be the favorite of all the most important people in Hong Kong. Some even speculated unkindly that she must have slept her way to the top.

Delia (not her real name) was exceptionally charming. She was also extremely capable and clever. But she too used feng shui to help her along and one of the things she loved most were windchimes. The main doors, both into her apartment block, as well as into her own luxurious penthouse in Hong Kong's Mid Levels faced NORTHWEST which was also her best sheng chi direction, according to the Pa Kua Lo Shu school of feng shui. She arranged to hang a large golden coloured windchime at both entrances.

The windchimes had eight rods and they created tinkling sounds throughout the day and night, thereby creating powerful feng shui.

And in her spacious bedroom, where the NW corner was she again hung a windchime, this time a smaller one ...

Delia went on to carve out a most illustrious career for herself, helped along by powerful people in the business community as well as in the Government ... she never lacked for powerful mentors.

The windchime that hung at the entrance of the apartment block must also have helped all her neighbors for many who lived in that particular apartment block also enjoyed a great deal of success.

Another method is to actually draw out the trigram CHIEN in the NW corner. This can be done in various ways. Simply incorporate three solid lines onto design of doors, windows and furniture that are placed in the NW corner. It is however vital to ensure that these three solid lines are not joined into other lines thereby signifying something else.

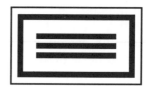

Two ways of using the trigram Chien to activate the NW corner of the room, on the left, painting it onto a sideboard placed in the NW, and on the right, a framed embroidery of Chien above an easy chair in the NW corner.

Activating the NW in effect activates your mentor luck. It is thus extremely helpful for career minded people who want an extra edge in climbing the corporate career.

SHENG ... the prosperity hexagram

Another very important symbol extracted from the I Ching is the hexagram Sheng, as in *sheng chi*, the dragon's cosmic breath. Chien is the trigram which signifies divine help from heaven. It is extremely *yang* in characteristic, and is thus suitable for life and activity. And Chien doubled, which is portrayed by six solid unbroken lines also signifies the same thing.

The hexagram SHENG meanwhile, is a combination of two different trigrams, the trigram SUN below, and the trigram KUN above. The meaning of SHENG is ascending, promotion or expansion. It thus has very auspicious significance. It is made up of the combination of earth (Kun) above and wood (Sun) below. Thus the plant is firmly rooted in the earth, and it is growing higher and higher. The season indicated is late Spring, a time of very rapid growth.

According to the I Ching's meaning this hexagram indicates that businesses will prosper like the growing trees that blossom and then bear fruit. This hexagram is also auspicious for marriages and for attracting mentor luck.

I first came across the use of this hexagram as a feng shui tool when attending a dinner hosted by a Shanghainese Bank. In Hong Kong, the Cantonese (who are in the majority) and the Shanghainese do not like each other much and they apparently keep very much to themselves, each dialect group not trusting the other much. Thus the Cantonese businessmen bank with Cantonese banks while the Shanghainese bank with Shanghainese banks !

Since I am a Malaysian Chinese banker, my allegiance was to neither and so I fraternized with both groups. I should explain to readers that banking, especially at the higher levels of management is a highly social occupation. Banks arrange money market lines with each other, and also exchange credit information with each other. Since I was new to Hong Kong at that time it was vital for me to get to know the senior management of especially the local banks. As such I invited them, and they invited me for dinner, at least once for us to exchange pleasantries and demonstrate goodwill to each other.

It was all part and parcel of the business of banking.
Usually these dinners (and sometimes lunch) are held in the private penthouses of these banks, and that occasion was no different.

175

I saw this Sheng symbol hanging in a glass frame above the entrance to the penthouse. Below the symbol were some words in Chinese, and it looked so unusual that I asked about it.

I did not get a direct reply, and any feng shui connotation to the symbol was not acknowledged. But being a keen student of the I Ching, I had recognized the symbol, so when I got home I checked out the meaning of the hexagram which was how I came to identify it as SHENG. Later I was told this symbol was widely used in Shanghai where it is regarded as an auspicious symbol.

Two years ago, a reader from Singapore wrote to me about this symbol. She did not know it as SHENG but she did draw it out. She asked whether this symbol, placed by her neighbor above the door facing her door would hurt her. Her letter told me that even in Singapore, where there are few Chinese of Shanghai origin, this symbol was being used.

I assured her that the symbol SHENG, unlike the protective Pa Kua does not send out killing energy. Indeed if anything it sends out *sheng chi,* the good auspicious breath, and is thus equally lucky for her since her neighbor's use of the symbol meant it was facing her front door.

This symbol can be placed anywhere in the house, inside or out, but is best displayed in the wealth corner, or at the entrance to businesses. In the wealth corner, ie the SOUTHEAST, the element is wood, which complements the hexagram's symbolic meaning perfectly. It can be drawn on wood and displayed, or it can be embroidered onto silk and framed.

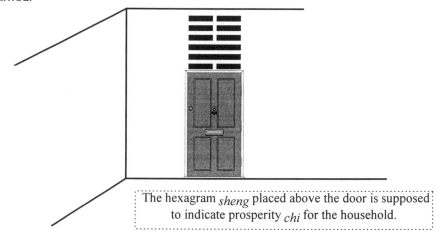

The hexagram *sheng* placed above the door is supposed to indicate prosperity *chi* for the household.

176

CHAPTER THIRTEEN
THE TUN'S WONDERFUL FENG SHUI
Activating the turtle for longevity and support

There is something quite mysteriously divine about feng shui. Again and again, it has been my good fortune to discover that those born with karmic good luck often get their feng shui right without trying, or even knowing anything about the science. Perhaps the most spectacular example of this has to be the case of a very dear and old friend of mine, someone whose friendship I consider a great honor simply because he epitomizes so much of the modern history of my country.

I first met Tun Omar Ong Yoke Lin when he was ambassador to Washington, and I was a very humble Govt. officer working then with the Malaysian Industrial Development Authority. I had been sent to New York to learn from a top PR Agency there, Ruder & Finn; to see how lobby groups worked, and observe how they positioned Malaysia as a wonderful new location for corporations looking for developing countries to site their new manufacturing operations. As Ambassador, the Tun was aware of the work being done by MIDA (then FIDA) and I was invited, along with other Malaysians in the States to an Embassy party.

Years later, after he had returned to Malaysia, I met him again when we became fellow directors on the Board of Hume Industries. I was working for the Hong Leong Group at that time and after the Group's successful takeover of Hume I joined the Board and there renewed my acquaintance with him. By then he had remarried after the death of his first wife, and through him I met his lovely wife Aishah, who over the years has become a bosom pal. I know of no kinder people than them both, and have seen how generous they are with the less privileged. Aishah does a lot of welfare work, and I had often remarked to myself how much they deserve their good fortune.

Both of them are devout Muslims and neither had even heard about feng shui until I started telling them about it. Quite out of curiosity on my part, I decided to investigate the feng shui of their home. I was convinced that someone like the Tun, who is now in his eighties, and who has had such a long and distinguished career, and had stayed so close to every single Prime Minister ... from the Tengku, through to Tun Razak, and then to Tun Hussein Onn, and now Dr. Mahathir must surely have excellent feng shui.

The Tun brilliantly symbolizes the equivalent of a learned *mandarin*, someone who had long ago crossed the dragon gates, and stayed there. It was not just his career that was distinguished. He has also been blessed with a wonderful family. He has a loving wife who obviously adores him and three brilliant children.

So I asked his permission to check out his feng shui. And this is what I discovered. First of all I checked out his directions and I discovered that the main front door into his house directly faced his *sheng chi* ie his best, most auspicious direction !

Their home is completely regular in shape and the swimming pool is placed at exactly the right location ! And as if that was not enough, quite by chance I discovered that in the North corner of his home, just in front of the main door, they had long ago built a very small pond, only about three feet in diameter, in which they had kept miniature tortoises. Because it was so long ago, and because the grounds are tended by the gardeners, they had long forgotten about its existence.

But this pond was supremely excellent feng shui indeed for in placing it in the North, they had unknowingly strengthened the water element, which of course represents wealth and prosperity ...

But the North is also the place of the black turtle in feng shui, a celestial creature which symbolizes support and backing from the highest authorities. By keeping tortoises there (and they are still alive), the symbolic significance was very effectively strengthened. Meanwhile, according to yet another school of feng shui, the North also represents the career corner ... is it any wonder then that he has had so much success in his long and distinguished career ? Is it any wonder that today, at the ripe old age of 80, he can sit back and enjoy his family and count amongst his closest friends all the most important people of. this country ? Surely there cannot be better feng shui than that ?

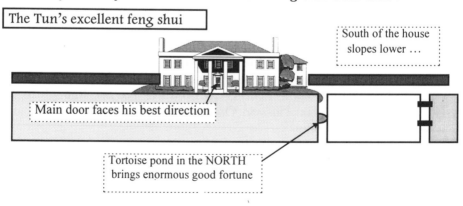

The Tun's excellent feng shui

South of the house slopes lower ...

Main door faces his best direction

Tortoise pond in the NORTH brings enormous good fortune

178

To those new to the science of feng shui, it is useful to understand that feng shui has neither spiritual nor religious connotations. It is instead a body of knowledge which lays down ancient guidelines on how best to harness the energy flows of the living Earth. Feng shui has thus a great deal to do with tapping earth luck from the environment, by cleverly regulating the so called *five elements* - water, fire, wood, earth and metal.

Sometimes, if one's luck is good, the feng shui of the home is correct even when nothing has been done to ensure it. There is harmony in the elements representative of the various corners, and environmental influences will be just right. How does one explain this ? I call it good karma ! I believe that one's good karma is enhanced when one does good deeds, although this is a philosophical belief, and not feng shui. I try not to make the mistake of mixing up the two concepts !

According to the Chinese view of the Universe, Mankind has three types of luck. The first kind of luck comes from heaven, and this describes the circumstances of birth and has to do with life's fortune over which you have no control. *Heaven luck* is sometimes referred to as fate ... in certain cultures, the belief is that fate cannot be changed. According to the Chinese, the belief is that though fate cannot be changed, it can be substantially modified either through the harnessing of *earth luck* ie feng shui, or through *mankind luck* which is in effect created by the person herself or himself. Thus if one has the fate to become the President of a country, the Chinese believe that it will very likely happen, but those who stay President for a long time and have a successful Presidency are those who also have good *earth luck* and *mankind luck,* Those who do not could well suffer misfortune even in the midst of the Presidency.

Thus in the old days emperors went to great lengths to ensure they had good feng shui, and there is plenty of evidence to indicate that feng shui was extensively applied in the building of the palaces in the Forbidden city in Beijing. Ancient feng shui texts are also replete with references to the feng shui of dynastic graves and imperial homes.

The symbolism of the turtle
Sharing my observations of the Tun's feng shui reminds me of another story that also features the turtle (more accurately a tortoise). This was during the days when   my home was in Bukit Tunku, then known as Kenny Hills. We stayed in quite luxurious quarters provided by my husband's employer.

Late one night, we were driving home when we saw, caught in our headlights, a small black tortoise crossing the road. We slowed down and watched it make its way slowly across the road., before moving on ... I would not have thought anything more about the incident but for the fact that the following day while playing with my dogs in the garden, I saw yet another small black tortoise just at the edge of my fence.

This was highly unusual since there were no streams or ponds nearby. Once again I dismissed the incident and did not give it another thought.

But a week later I was presented with a pair of tiny miniature tortoises by a friend. It was left at my home, and I thought they were very cute but really I had no use for them at all. It did not occur to me there could be any hidden significance to the fact that three times in two weeks I had met up with these creatures.

I gave the tortoises to Soraya, an old friend from Penang who had recently married and moved to live in Kuala Lumpur. She had a small pond in her link house in Petaling Jaya, and she welcomed the tortoises. I remember her telling me they were *just perfect* for the pond and for her new baby to play with ...

That was more than twenty years ago. Today Soraya is Puan Sri Soraya. She no longer lives in PJ having moved to a palatial new mansion in Ukay Heights some years ago. When I saw her last I inquired about the tortoises. Apparently shortly after I gave them to her, someone had casually told her that tortoises were good luck, so she had continued to keep them.

"*They now live in that pond over there*" she said pointing to a very well kept pond by the side of the garden. I took out my compass to get my bearings, and sure enough, just as I suspected, the pond had been located in a most auspicious location - the Southeast actually, which is of course the wealth corner. No wonder they are so wealthy !

Soraya's husband does not believe in feng shui, and I do not want to embarrass them by revealing their real identities. But it seems that I have now come across two people whose friendship with the symbolic turtle has given them some sort of divine helping hand.

I often wonder whether I would have been richer, and more successful if I had not been so foolish as to give away the tortoises. They had come right up to my doorstep, and I had turned them away !

I can only conclude that it was not meant to be, and indeed, when I related this story to Yap Cheng Hai, we had a good laugh over it.

It was not your luck then to keep the tortoises, he chuckled. But we looked up references to the turtle in his store of feng shui texts, and he confirmed that the turtle was indeed a wonderful feng shui symbol of prosperity and longevity. In short the turtle is representative of great good luck.

The turtle is a longevity symbol, one of many in the Chinese pantheon of symbols. It is also one of the four celestial creatures that make up the animal symbolism of feng shui practice, the other three being the dragon, the tiger and the phoenix.

Because of its slow and steady characteristic, the turtle is said to provide solid and long lasting support, and due to its tenacious character, it is rightly placed in the North to withstand the cold winds that blow from that direction.

The turtle is also famous for the part it plays in the evolution of so called *Lo Shu magic,* the placement of numbers in the nine sector grid which is such a large component of Compass feng shui. Thus those who want to ensure support in their work, career and business would do well to incorporate turtle symbolism in their feng shui.

There are several ways of introducing the turtle into your home feng shui. Keep a pair of live miniature tortoises in a small pond ... they are easily available in any aquarium shop. Feed them with *kangkong* or other fresh leafy vegetables, and let them have a supply of slow moving water.

Or look for a model of a turtle ... the kind you find in any garden shop which sells all weather models of birds, water jars and decorative pots. (There is such a shop in Old Klang road in Kuala Lumpur) ... then place the turtle at either one of the following suitable locations:

- The North corner or side of your garden (see sketch on next page)

- The back of the house, especially if the land there is slightly elevated. This will symbolize support for the residents.

Place turtle here

Or you can hang a picture of a turtle behind your desk at work, or in the North corner of your living room. This activates the vital support which we need to succeed in our endeavors. This is shown in the sketch below.

Picture of turtle hung on North wall, or behind you in the office. This is good feng shui.

CHAPTER FOURTEEN
FISHY STORIES
.... of arrowanas, carps and goldfish

I have so many stories I can tell you about the wonderful luck that fish can bring to a household. I myself benefited handsomely from the five arrowanas I installed onto a gigantic aquarium I built into one wall of my living room, and I have become a firm advocate of keeping fish, or if that is not possible to hang paintings of good luck fish.

When I moved to my new apartment in Hong Kong, I wanted to make enough money to retire and come home to Malaysia, so I decided it was time to put prosperity feng shui to work for me.

I had a huge aquarium built onto one wall of my living room. I had been advised to keep five arrowanas, and since these fish grew quickly, the tank would have to be huge. I also knew that at balance had to be maintained. Otherwise the water would drown me. So I simultaneously knocked down the dividing wall between the living and dining rooms. I also installed a full length wall mirror to reflect the dining table. All this had the effect of substantially enlarging the living area, and the large aquarium did not look so large after all ...

The five arrowanas which brought me prosperity luck

It was during those years when I lived with my arrowanas, that I successfully acquired the Dragon Seed group which made me and my partners a lot of money ... enough to allow me to stop working.

When I packed up to come home, I was offered a small fortune for my Arrowanas. By then they had grown to about eighteen inches in length and their scales had taken on a delightfully silver pink hue ... a sure sign of prosperity, according to feng shui experts ... it was irrelevant that I had given them a bit of help by feeding them on a diet of live goldfish ! I turned down the offer and freed them in the friendly waters of Stanley reservoir. I felt that giving them their freedom was a small gesture of appreciation which would also enhance my own karma ...

Mine is not the only positive experience with arrowanas. One of my feng shui friends in Hong Kong who had given me the tip about these feng shui fish had related the story of a client of his who had kept a single arrowana, and had gone on to become one of the largest garment manufacturers in the colony. I also saw a two feet long arrowana in Bangkok of a different variety. This one had a double ended tail fin, and it was a fish which the owner claimed could talk ! The owner, a successful gem dealer had kept the fish for eighteen years. He claimed the fish had brought him so much luck, he loved it more than his wife !

During my days as a banker, I also saw the inside of many local banking boardrooms and offices of CEOs and one of the things I noticed was that they kept aquariums in their own office. A particularly beautiful aquarium I saw was at the office of Sun Hung Kai Securities. At that time the patriarch who founded the company was still alive, and I have no idea if his son, who has taken over as the head of the company still keeps the aquarium. But Mr. Fung had the most stunning goldfish.

It was a rare variety and I was told they were the type that were kept by the emperors of China. These goldfish (quite enormous in size, and very imperial looking) had crowns above their heads and sported very long flowing and gleaming fins and tails. They wiggled as they swam and were fed only on the best type of fish food. There were nine goldfish in the aquarium, eight in glorious red/gold and one in gleaming black. I was informed that old Mr. Fung loved his goldfish. He attributed much of his excellent business luck to them. He was of course also a stunningly brilliant entrepreneur, much respected in the colony.

When I returned to live in my old house in Kuala Lumpur, I was at first keen to go in search of arrowanas, with the intention of repeating my business luck ... but on second thoughts shelved the idea because my Kuala Lumpur home already had a fish pond which had been there for many years ago. In the pond were my husband's pride and joy, his collection of Japanese carp, or *koi*, which themselves are also regarded as very auspicious fish.

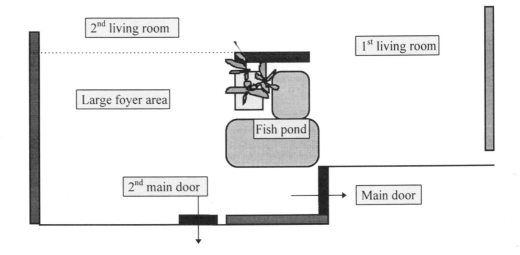

Our collection of *koi* are not the expensive ones, being locally bred rather than imported. But they are just as lucky !

I decided that too much water and too many fish might be excessive. When I renovated the house, I brought the fish pond into the house (it had been located outside the house) and created a sort of air well, allowing rain water into the pond each time it rained.

I should mention that airwells inside the home are NOT a bad thing from a feng shui perspective. But ideally, they should not be located in the center of the house since the center is be the *heart of the home* and should be a room of substance (ideally the dining room), rather than be an empty place.
My fishpond catch *waters from heaven* and create lots of favorable *sheng chi* which then flow auspiciously through the home ... it is also on the left hand side of the two main doors !

Aquarium of guppies bring job offers galore

We go skiing with a young Malaysian couple, who live and work in London. Tom and Sharon are both keen feng shui enthusiasts. Tom is a computer expert who transformed my Compass Pa Kua Lo Shu formula into a computer software which allows quick and easy feng shui consultations to be produced according to individual dates of birth.

I spend time with them when I go to London because Tom serves the most delicious *salmon sashimi.* He wakes up early in the morning and motors down to Billingsgate to buy one enormous fresh salmon which he cuts up so expertly it would put many a Japanese chef to shame. On one such occasion, Sharon casually asked me what they could do to improve their career prospects. Sharon and Tom are alumni of Cambridge University. She was with the Malaysian Timber Council, enduring a certain amount of frustration while Tom held a job with a Saudi publishing company, taking care of their computers and churning out web sites on the then still fledgling Internet. They lived comfortably in a flat off busy Oxford street, and can be perceived to be enjoying life. But something must have been amiss to prompt Sharon's request.

So I looked around the living room of the flat, and casually told them to activate their career corner ! From my bag I took out my traveling compass. We found out they were both East group people, with North being their best direction and South the second best. That they belonged to the same group accounted for their compatibility. As East group people, activating the career corner, ie North would be doubly beneficial since North is auspicious for east group people.

Activate the North of this room I told them.   The North is represented by the trigram KAN, a strong unbroken yang line sandwiched between two broken yin lines. The element of the North is water. So that what they needed was a small aquarium to be placed in the North corner.

And there the matter ended ... except that some months later I got a call from Tom who told me he had a dilemma. He had been approached by several people all wanting to discuss job offers with him. Three in particular looked interesting, as all three came with the promise of more money, one of which represented almost a tripling of his income, while another came with a seat on the Board. He was now very uncertain as to which job offer to take, and even whether he should leave his present job, because they were reluctant to lose him, and they too had indicated they were prepared to give him a big raise.

In the end Tom took several months to decide. In the meanwhile I visited them again as business takes me frequently to London, and guess what I saw in their living room but a very cute, well lighted aquarium, the type you see in Harrods - very modern and pretty. It was a medium sized aquarium, not too big nor too small, and inside were a school of tiny little guppies swimming happily up and down the tube shaped aquarium, while tiny little bubbles moved upwards in a never ending flow. A wonderful energizer indeed for the North corner ...

There is little doubt in my mind or theirs that the guppies caused a major change in Tom's career fortunes. Today Tom has taken the job with the US firm CISCO, the largest supplier of Internet hardware in the world ... He is based in Brussels now, makes an excellent income and according to him, is extremely happy. Except for the weekend commuting to London to see his wife which has now become a frustrating feature of their life. Sharon meanwhile has left her job with the Timber Council and is busy, successfully running her own business.

I am sure it is the mirror in their bedroom, (this caught my attention last summer. I had to pass through their room to enjoy their small garden which comes alive with flowers and plants in the summer) as well as the TV monitor directly facing their bed which seems to be causing this enforced separation ... but we shall have to see the effect of any changes being made to these offending bedroom features.

But the guppies have done their job, and I would strongly advise those who want to give their careers a lift to try this method of activating their career feng shui. Any small fishbowl will do the job, like the goldfish bowl shown here. Just keep the water well aerated with bubbling oxygen and let the fish bring you some smashing good fortune.

Simulating the dragon gate

According to ancient Chinese legend, the humble carp swims upstream until it reaches the Dragon Gates, and with a mighty heave it jumps across the gate and those who make it are transformed into dragons. Those that do not make it have to turn back and be content with being carp all their life ... except that unlike normal carps, those who failed bore the stamp of failure, a round red dot on their foreheads. So do not keep carp with a red dot on its head as it means failure.

In the old days, scholars who successfully passed the Imperial examinations and who went on to carve successful careers for themselves as mandarins, judges or as court advisors to the emperors were likened to having successfully passed the Dragon Gate.

Over time this gate has come to signify the attainment of power and authority, and those presently carving out careers for themselves in politics, in the judiciary or in the civil service would benefit hugely by having the dragon feature in their office or home feng shui.

Displaying the symbol of the Dragon Carp

I have been told that former Hong Kong dragon lady, Baroness Lydia Dunn, who for many years was described as Hong Kong's most powerful woman, possesses a pair of antique wooden carvings that show the carp being transformed into a dragon ie with a dragon head and a fish body !

More recently I was told that the present dragon lady of Hong Kong, the extremely popular Anson Chan who is also Hong Kong's most senior civil servant being the colony's Chief Secretary also has this dragon gate feature in the feng shui of her home. I do not know if these stories about two of Hong Kong's most distinguished ladies are true, but I would not be surprised if they were.

Lydia Dunn has left Hong Kong to live in the UK with her husband, Anson Chan is widely tipped to be the first Chinese appointed chief executive of Hong Kong in 1997. She will certainly continue to be a powerful voice in post 1997 Hong Kong !

I myself was presented with a miniature of the dragon gate many years ago when I first started working for the Hong Leong group. It was given to me by a Taiwanese friend who had been at Business School with me at Harvard.

Ben came to visit me in KL and had brought along the gift, which he thought was most appropriate to wish me good luck in my new job. For years, the lacquered wooden item stood, almost ignored in my living room.

At that time I did not know of the legend associated with dragon gates, nor did I appreciate their significance, but by having it displayed in my living room, it surely must have helped me along my career with Hong Leong to no small degree.

I know of a very successful businessman in Singapore who decorated the top corners of the main entrance to his home with a pair of wooden dragon/carps. He is a well known industrial tycoon, and he once told me that the dragon/carps had been placed there as much for their aesthetic value as for their feng shui significance.

Each time I walk out of my house, he joked, I become a dragon . I become more courageous !

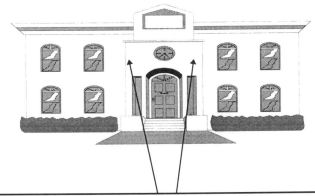

The dragon/carp, with the head of a dragon and the body of a carp placed at the top corners of the main door signifies crossing the dragon gate and brings success to businessmen and politicians

What is amazing is that he has three sons, and the eldest has now entered politics in Singapore and looks to have embarked on his own road to power and glory. The sons still live in the family mansion, and there is no doubt they too are benefiting from their father's excellent feng shui.

Crossing the Dragon Gate to wealth & power

Legend has it that when the humble carp swims through the Celestial Dragon Gates, it becomes transformed into a dragon. In olden days, scholars who passed the Imperial exams to qualify for powerful appointments in the emperor's court were likened to the carp ascending these heavenly gates. In those days, court advisors had to pass examinations that required knowledge of China's Classics, one of which was the I Ching. Those with lofty ambitions to get the ear of the emperor, or to become powerful State officials had to possess the ability to interpret the predictions revealed through the I Ching, and to also have knowledge of feng shui.

In ancient China, dragon (and phoenix) motifs were used as decorative features in the homes of the rich and the influential. These appeared in paintings, on vases, on porcelain and also carved as subjects on doors, ceilings and gates.
The legendary Dragon Gates or *lung men*, are said to have been located at a mountain pass along the Yellow river and were supposedly erected in the days of the Xia dynasty.

Striving to ascend the dragon gates ... *deng lung men* ... therefore represents the cherished hope of commoners who were not born into rich or influential families, since this was seen as the only way they could become *dragons*.

Carvings of Dragon Gates can still be seen in old mansions or temples in Singapore, Hong Kong, Taiwan and China. These generally form part of the roof's architectural structure, and frequently show several carps attempting to cross the gates which are guarded by two majestic dragons.

CHAPTER FIFTEEN
POISON ARROWS CAUSE HAVOC
Sometimes, even a tree can create shar chi ...

I can say that almost every case of bad feng shui I have witnessed over the years have been caused by *secret poison arrows*; and much of feng shui has to do with recognizing these arrows and dealing with the *shar chi* emanating from these arrows. Most times, however, it is easy to miss recognizing these structures as the harmful *arrows* they are, unless one is sufficiently experienced.

This was exactly what happened to me during the early years of my marriage. My husband and I wanted to start a family, but no matter how hard we tried, I could not get pregnant, and in the end we resigned ourselves to being childless. In those days we were living in quarters, and feng shui was something quite alien to us.

It was only years later after much damage had been done to our marriage that we discovered our house was being hit by *shar chi* that was created by a single casuarina tree which stood ten yards directly in front of our main door. It was Yap Cheng Hai who told us about it. He also told me quite categorically that as long as we stayed there we would never have a child, and our marriage would also disintegrate ! As it turned out he was right for our marriage did get bad, and we did not have a child until after moving out to our present house ...

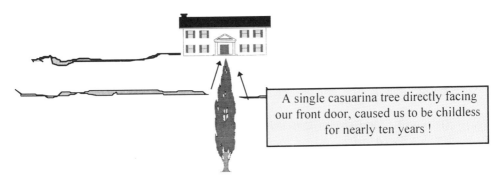

A single casuarina tree directly facing our front door, caused us to be childless for nearly ten years !

Getting rid of bad *shar chi* is often a creative exercise. But certain types of arrows are easier to deal with than others. Before one can get started however, it is necessary to first learn how to spot the presence of these hidden, and sometimes symbolic *arrows.*

In the environment that surrounds your home, all kinds of structures can represent harmful *poison arrows* ... The edge of a neighbor's house; a straight road directly in front of the house; a single tree trunk; a transmission tower; a cross structure caused by escalators or facades of buildings from across the road; a pointed roof line, and in fact anything that looks sharp, pointed and hostile ! Some of these   harmful structures are illustrated below. If your home or office faces any of these structures, do try strenuously to block them off from your view.

EXAMPLES OF POISON ARROWS
IN THE ENVIRONMENT

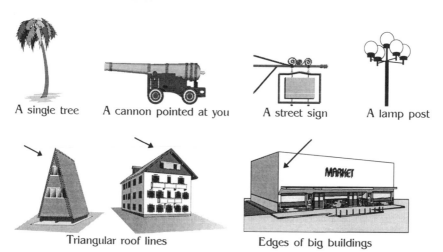

A single tree   A cannon pointed at you   A street sign   A lamp post

Triangular roof lines   Edges of big buildings

The examples of *poison arrows* shown above are usually harmful only if they are directly hitting at the main front door. In feng shui it is important to understand that *shar* chi travels in straight lines. Thus only if the structure is directly hitting your door, will the *shar chi* enter the home. If it is not, the structure is not harmful.

If they do face your main door, the best way to deal with them is to reflect them back with a <u>mirror.</u> The problem is that if the mirror is too small, it will not be sufficiently powerful to counter the harmful effects of the *shar chi.* The Chinese often use a <u>Pa Kua</u> with a mirror in the center and this symbol is regarded as being more potent.

Personally however I have discovered that the best way of dealing with these massive poison arrows is to re-orientate the door away from the offending structure.

If that is not possible, try growing a clump of trees. Select trees that have good foliage cover so that they effectively block off the offending structure. It works if the structure is completely cutoff and cannot be seen from the house altogether.

Sometimes building a wall also helps, except that the wall should not be too close to the main door. In fact, good feng shui requires there to be at least some empty space in front of the main door. Any wall or clump of trees that is too near the main door results in *chi* getting blocked. Empty space in front of the main door also represents the bright hall that is said to represent such excellent feng shui.

BLOCKING OFF POISON ARROWS

 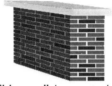 

Grow a clump of trees   Build a wall to separate   Change front door direction

Poison arrows in the environment that are caused by transmission towers, the chimney of a large factory or power plant, or some other gigantic structure, are extremely difficult to combat. This is because the negative harmful energy that is created is much too strong, and certainly cannot be deflected with tiny mirrors or even clumps of trees.

Perhaps the best way of deflecting such energy is to symbolically meet energy with energy, and this can be done by using a canon. Someone I met recently lived very close to a transmission tower, which stood huge and threatening on a hill by the side of her house. It was not facing her main door, but her twelve year old son became seriously ill and she suspected it was due to the presence of the tower. Since she could not move out I advised her to install a canon by the side of her house, and to aim the canon at the transmission tower.

Since she lived in Sarawak it was easy to find a canon. Soon after, her son recovered and she also feels a great deal better. Perhaps negative vibrations set up by big structures cause the environment to become unbalanced. Whatever it is, the canon is one object that is very effective in dealing with massive structures that symbolically *threaten* the home.

Inside the home, *shar chi* is often caused by exposed overhead beams, protruding corners, stand alone square columns, the pointed edges of cupboards as well as any structure that is pointed, sharp or triangular.

Spotting these features is actually very easy feng shui, and most people should have no problem diagnosing the presence of poison arrows inside the home. Sharp edges of walls and furniture can be softened with plants while the poisonous breath of overhead beams can be deflected with windchimes.

In addition to structural and built in features which are harmful, it is also advisable to be on the lookout for decorative items which could also be inadvertently causing feng shui problems. Such things as guns and cross swords that are quite commonly found in the old ancestral homes of the landed gentry in England, or in the homes of hunters can sometimes be exceedingly harmful, and are best removed.

| Do not hang cross swords above the door. The pointed blades send out negative breath ! | Displaying prize guns and pistols in the home is simply asking for trouble, especially when they are kept in glass cupboards and are clearly visible. They could well cause misfortunes to occur. | Knives and blades, scissors and other sharp items are best kept inside drawers. These objects emit *shar chi* as well. |

Remember that by themselves bad feng shui features might not do that much harm, but over time, and when accumulated with a great many other things going wrong, problems can and often do start to magnify unless you take steps to make some corrections ... so even for non believers who might be tempted to dismiss feng shui as frivolous, I always say, no one can really afford to be totally ignorant about the defensive aspects of feng shui practice. My contention is that, one does not need to go too deep into the science of feng shui, if one is not keen to do so. Just knowing how to recognize and deflect poison arrows is sometimes sufficient as it then ensures that at least you do not suffer from bad feng shui.

SUMMARY OF FENG SHUI POISON ARROWS

 | Downward arrows are caused by exposed overhead beams |

| Level arrows are caused by edges of walls, cabinets & furniture |

 | Straight arrows are caused by long corridors and straight roads |

| Multiple arrows are caused by X shaped structures like escalators. |

 | V shaped arrows are caused by staircases, edges or hostile objects like cannons, single trees, lampposts or poles. |

All of these *arrows* emanate *shar chi*, the poisonous breath. You must be on the lookout for them. Sometimes they are not at first obvious, and requires an experienced eye. But once you develop an awareness for them, you will be able to spot them ... it comes with practice !
The best way to handle them is to move out of the line of fire ie move your door, move your bed or move your chair so that the *arrow* is no longer aimed at the door, the bed or the chair. If doing this means having to spend too much money, then the next best method is to place some kind of object which successfully blocks off the offending structure. In feng shui, cures usually involve deflecting, blocking or dissolving.

Thus screens can block off *shar chi*; Plants can dissolve *shar chi* Mirrors can deflect *shar chi*; Wind chimes and bells dissolve *shar chi* Curtains and Room dividers block off *shar chi*; Lights dissolve *shar chi*, Once you have diagnosed the source of the problem, you can decide on the best way of dealing with it .. either to deflect, to block or to dissolve the bad poisonous breath that is causing the bad feng shui.

SELECTING FENG SHUI CURES :

In selecting the cure you wish to use try and match the element of the cure used with the compass location of the problem.

Use windchimes to counter the effect of overhead beams, and protruding corners. The metal ones are very effective when hung in the North West and West sectors/corners of rooms, since the representative element in these corners is metal.

Curtains are very effective when used to block out bad views of structures that create shar chi. Use the heavy drapes or chintz curtains. They are effective in any corner of the house but it is not a bad idea to select colors according to the compass directions. Thus white for West/Northwest; Green for east/Southeast; red for South; Black or blue for North; and yellow for Southwest and Northeast.

Lights are powerful antidotes for all sorts of feng shui problems. They can also be used to dissolve *shar chi* caused by sharp edges and protruding corners. Especially when placed in the South corners of rooms, or of the home, lights are excellent for transforming *yin* energy into *yang* energy; and *shar chi* into *sheng chi*.

The reflective power of mirrors has the effect of sending shar chi back to where it came from. Thus placing a mirror in front of offending structures can sometimes be extremely effective. Mirrors also have other uses in feng shui, but it is advisable to be careful, e.g. they should never be used in the bedroom, especially if they reflect the bed ...

Plants are wonderful feng shui tools. Because they always symbolize growth, they are also excellent energizers. As a cure, they are good for softening edges,. They block off shar chi, and absorb much of the poisonous breath emanated. Plants are thus good to have around, particularly in the East, South and Southeast corners of the home, or of individual rooms.

Use screens to block off bad views, or to break the flow of *shar chi* caused by three doors in a row. Choose screens which have pleasant scenery, or better yet look out for those which portray good fortune or longevity symbols. Display them straight rather than wavy as this will themselves causes poison arrows.

Combating *shar chi* with a cannon

I usually discourage friends from using the cannon to combat *shar chi*. This is because the cannon is a very powerful feng shui tool. It creates massive *shar chi* and should only be used as a last resort.

In down town Kuala Lumpur, there is a building located directly opposite the Boustead Building which has an offensive feng shui feature. This was two escalators that formed a massive X in the foyer of the building. This X sent *shar chi* across the road and adversely affected the Boustead Building. Apparently the business of Boustead suffered, and after seeking feng shui advice, they erected a large antique cannon by the side of their entrance, and this cannon aimed directly at the escalators.

The cannon successfully demolished the *shar chi* created by the X shaped escalators, but in the process, it generated its own killing breath which in turn, affected the business of the occupants in the building across the road. To counter the cannon, they then placed a round mirror to reflect away the cannon's killing breath ... The feng shui battle between the two buildings continues ... and those who wish, may take a drive along Jalan Raja Chulan to have a look at the offending escalators, the beautiful cannon, and the round mirror ! This is illustrated here.

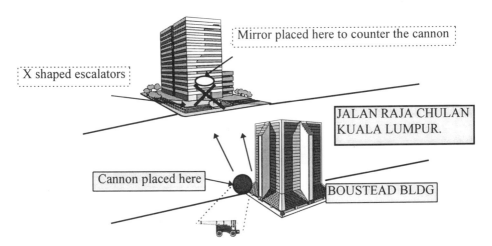

Mirror placed here to counter the cannon

X shaped escalators

JALAN RAJA CHULAN
KUALA LUMPUR.

Cannon placed here

BOUSTEAD BLDG

I do not believe the <u>small</u> mirror is a match for the life size cannon. It would be a better solution to place another cannon to face the cannon. This would have balanced the energies. There are also *male* and *female* cannons, or *yin and yang* cannons. Matching the *yin* with a *yang* will be an ideal way of dissolving the *shar chi* of a cannon.

Combating cannon with a large mirror

In another case which also features the cannon, there was a woman who was given two cannons as a gift, and she placed the two cannons in front of her house. Unfortunately the cannons inadvertently hit at the front doors of her neighbors. One hit at the home of a very high Government official, and within three months, the gentleman lost his high powered job. The other cannon hit at the home of a politician, and he too was voted out shortly after ... When she was told that her cannons could have been the cause of her neighbors misfortunes, she immediately removed the cannons and instead of pointing them at the neighbors in front of her house, she moved them to the back. Unfortunately, in doing so the cannons now pointed to the valley below, where there were also houses.

The house in the valley that was the most directly hit was occupied by a timber merchant, and shortly thereafter his business suffered a major loss. When he realized that the cannon from above could be the cause of his misfortune, he immediately installed a mirror to reflect the cannon. This had the effect of deflecting the killing energy back to its source, and coincidence or not, within six months two maids died in the house with the cannon. The mirror used had been a very large mirror ! Cannons should be treated with great respect and care.

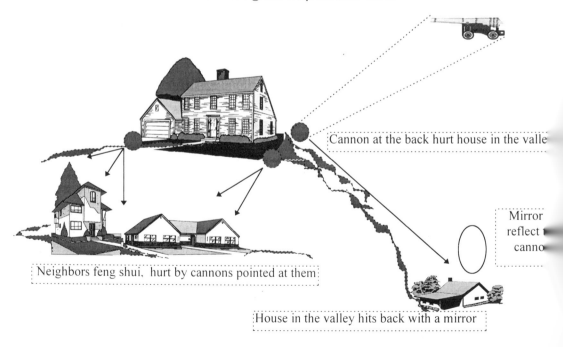

Cannon at the back hurt house in the valle

Mirror
reflect
canno

Neighbors feng shui, hurt by cannons pointed at them

House in the valley hits back with a mirror

CLOSING NOTES

The compilation of stories that make up this book offer a diverse look at the many different ways feng shui's auspicious *sheng chi* and the killing *shar chi* works. This hopefully has added depth to the reader's perception of feng shui practice.

It should also be obvious that there are many dimensions of feng shui practice ... I have included stories of good and bad feng shui; as well as stories with happy and unhappy endings. There are also stories from China, some of which have become the stuff of legends and folk tales

I was also excited at being able to include the section on the Forbidden City. This evidence of the imperial use of feng shui is wonderful testimony of feng shui's acceptance amongst the ruling classes throughout China's history. It is probably this, more than anything else which has enabled the science to have survived all these centuries.

The prime objectives of this book were two fold; firstly, I wanted to flesh out feng shui theory with the colours and dimensions of its practice. Secondly, I also wanted to provide a personal testimony of the role of feng shui in my own life. Hence I have included chapters on some of my more colorful experiences with feng shui.

I hope after reading this collection of stories, those who want to tap into the auspicious energies of good feng shui can now go about the practice with greater confidence.

There is much common sense involved when it comes to arranging your living space in a balanced and harmonious manner. And in truth, you do not need to get an expert in to do your feng shui. It is better and more meaningful if you try doing it yourself .... Feng shui is about common sense, but it is not intuitive. Feng shui is based on a set body of guidelines. Learn these guidelines well, then put them to good use by applying them in your own living space ... excellence does come with practice, as will insights into the theories behind the science.

Just remember, if I can do it, YOU can do it TOO !!

Lillian Too
October 1996

About the author

Lillian Too lives in Malaysia where she heads her own publishing and investment company. She is the author of several best selling books including her ever popular feng shui series. In recent months she has also come out with the full color COMPLETE ILLUSTRATED GUIDE TO FENG SHUI published by Element Books UK, USA and Australia, and which had its world wide release in October this year.

Lillian holds an MBA degree from the Harvard Business School, Boston, USA. She had a varied and successful career in the corporate worlds of Malaysia and Hong Kong, becoming in the early Eighties, the first woman in Malaysia to head a publicly listed company, and later the first woman in Asia to become CEO of a bank. She also successfully packaged a leveraged buyout of the Dragon Seed department store group in Hong Kong and became its Executive Chairman in 1987. She has since sold out and returned to Malaysia. Lillian is married and has one daughter.

Trade Inquiries may be addressed to the following:

UK & EUROPE
MILLBANK BOOKS
The Courtyard, The Old Monastery,
Bishops Stortford, Hertfordshire,
CM23 2PE, United Kingdom.
Tel: 44 1279 655 233
Fax: 44 1279 655 244

AUSTRALIA & NEW ZEALAND
ORIENTAL PUBLICATIONS
16 Market Street,
Adelaide South Australia 5000,
Australia.
Tel: 618 212 6055
Fax: 618 410 0863